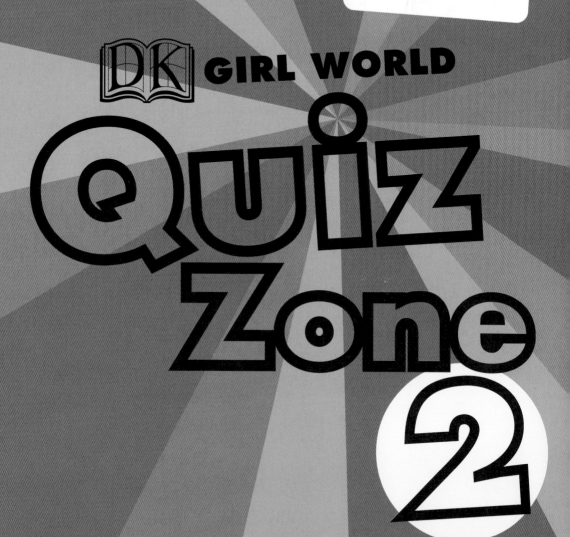

DK **GIRL WORLD**

Quiz Zone

2

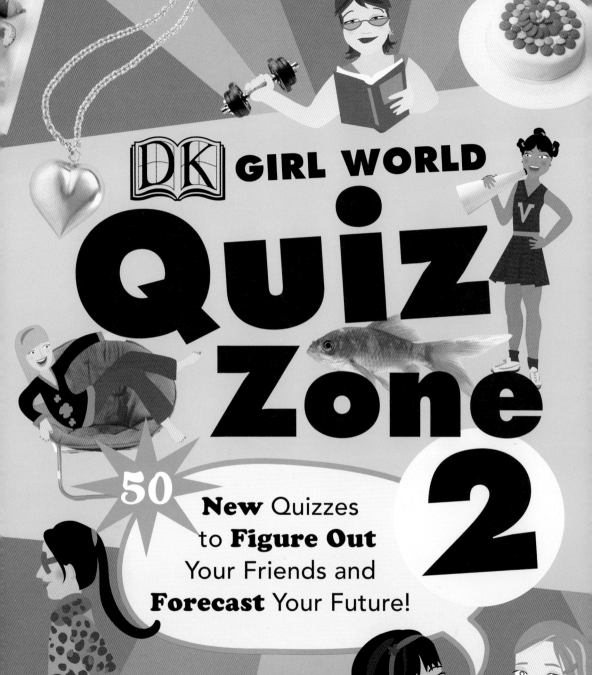

DK GIRL WORLD
Quiz Zone
2

50 **New** Quizzes to **Figure Out** Your Friends and **Forecast** Your Future!

by **Michelle Hainer**
Illustrations by
Georgia Rucker

DK

LONDON, NEW YORK, MUNICH,
MELBOURNE, AND DELHI

Senior Editor Elizabeth Hester
Designer Jessica Park
Managing Art Editor Michelle Baxter
Art Director Dirk Kaufman
Publishing Director Beth Sutinis
Production Ivor Parker
DTP Coordinator Kathy Farias

DOWNTOWN BOOKWORKS INC.

PRODUCED BY DOWNTOWN BOOKWORKS INC.
President Julie Merberg
Senior Vice President Patty Brown
Editor Sarah Parvis

DESIGNED BY GEORGIA RUCKER DESIGN
Designer and Illustrator Georgia Rucker

First published in the United States in 2007 by
DK Publishing, 375 Hudson Street
New York, New York 10014
07 08 09 10 11 10 9 8 7 6 5 4 3 2 1

Published in Great Britain by Dorling Kindersley Limited.

A catalog record for this book is available from the
Library of Congress.

ISBN 978-0-7566-2670-9

DK books are available at special discounts when
purchased in bulk for sales promotions, premiums,
fund-raising, or educational use. For details, contact:
DK Publishing Special Markets, 375 Hudson Street, New
York, New York 10014 or SpecialSales@dk.com.

Color reproduction by Colourscan, Singapore
Printed and bound in China by Leo Paper Products Ltd.

Discover more at
www.dk.com

Contents

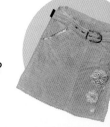

Are You **A POSITIVE PERSON**?

Do you try to look on the bright side of life? Even when skies are gray?

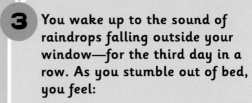

1 You ran for school secretary and really wanted to win but didn't. When you heard the news, you:

a. weren't surprised. You have the worst luck in the world.

b. felt sad. But it would have required hours of meetings and school service, which you can now spend playing soccer or hanging out with friends.

c. shrugged it off. Some things just aren't meant to be.

2 Your best friend has a crush on the most popular boy in school and talks about him constantly. The next time she mentions his name, you say:

a. "I am sure he'll like you back. There is no way he could miss how fabulous you are."

b. "Want me to find out if he has a girlfriend?"

c. "You'll never have a chance with him. He only dates sporty girls."

3 You wake up to the sound of raindrops falling outside your window—for the third day in a row. As you stumble out of bed, you feel:

a. happy. At least the plants and trees are getting some much-needed water.

b. a little annoyed. Your hair gets really frizzy in this weather, but your rain boots sure are cute.

c. miserable. The thought of going outside makes you want to crawl back into bed and pull the covers over your head.

4 You studied really hard for a history test. As you walk out of class, you:

a. just know you failed. There are way too many facts in history for you to possibly remember them all.

b. think you did OK, but there were a few questions you didn't know the answers to.

c. feel really good. The questions seemed easy because you were so well prepared.

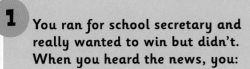

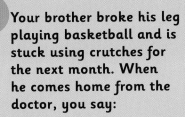

5 Your brother broke his leg playing basketball and is stuck using crutches for the next month. When he comes home from the doctor, you say:

a. "Well, you might not be a starting member of the team for a while, but I'm sure you'll be able to play again."

b. "Just hope your basketball career isn't over for good. I don't know what you'd do without sports."

c. "You're really strong, so you're going to be back on the court in no time. And in the meantime, Mom is totally going to wait on you hand and foot!"

6 You just found out your dad lost his job. When you hear the news, you:

a. know that your dad will find work. While he's looking, at least you'll get to see more of him.

b. start rationing your food. It won't be long before you're waiting in line at the local soup kitchen.

c. are definitely worried and begin searching online for a job so that you can help out if things get tough.

7 One of your friends really wants to be a professional ballerina and practices constantly—leaving her little time to hang out with you. When she breaks plans again, you:

a. tell her she's wasting her time in the dance studio. She'll never be good enough to go pro.

b. feel hurt but don't say anything. She's promised she won't forget about you when she's famous.

c. admire her dedication. She has a goal, and she'll do whatever she can to achieve it.

8 When things don't go your way, you:

a. let yourself be sad for a little while but try not to feel sorry for yourself for long.

b. realize that you can't get everything you want and try to focus on what you do have.

c. wonder when your streak of bad luck is going to end.

ANSWERS

1 a=1 b=3 c=2
2 a=3 b=2 c=1
3 a=3 b=2 c=1
4 a=1 b=2 c=3
5 a=2 b=1 c=3
6 a=3 b=1 c=2
7 a=1 b=2 c=3
8 a=2 b=3 c=1

20–24 points

ACCENTUATE THE POSITIVE

You can see the silver lining in even the darkest storm cloud. You don't let yourself be negative and always make the best of any situation. Your friends count on you to make them feel better when they're down.

14–19 points

POSITIVE TO A POINT

You believe in the power of positive thinking, but when something crummy happens, you do allow yourself to wallow in self-pity for a bit. Then, you start realizing how good your life really is, and that's what makes you feel better.

8–13 points

NEGATIVE NELLY

Can you see the good in anything? You have no faith that good things will come to you, so you spend most of your time trying to convince others that the same is true for them. Try to focus on the upside of life. Nobody likes a downer.

What Will Your Dream Wedding Look Like?

Distant destination or hometown affair?
What will your wedding be like?

1 You go shopping for your dress and instantly fall for the one with:

a. a full skirt and long, lacy train.

b. delicate beading.

c. the light blue fabric. Who says brides always have to wear white?

2 You want your bridesmaids to:

a. look identical in full-length strapless gowns. They'll wear their hair up and don matching silver strappy sandals.

b. wear simple knee-length dresses in a spring color like pale pink or mint green.

c. wear whatever they want, just as long as they show it to you first. You want them to be comfortable.

3 When you imagine the flowers at your wedding, you always see:

a. lots of lush red roses.

b. hand-tied bouquets made of tulips.

c. vibrant, colorful bunches with lots of greens mixed in.

4 Where will you have your wedding ceremony?

a. In a church or other house of worship

b. In your parents' beautiful outdoor garden

c. On an exotic beach, far from home

5 You're at the bakery tasting several wedding cake samples. Which do you choose?

a. A round, three-tiered, vanilla cake with a delicious fruit filling

b. Carrot cake with cream cheese frosting—it's your favorite

c. Individual raspberry-filled chocolate cupcakes with white icing for each of your guests

6 You've sent out your invitations. What do they look like?

a. Scrolls that unwind to reveal elegant wording announcing your impending marriage

b. Textured ivory squares with the time, date, and location printed in calligraphy

c. You didn't send formal invitations. Your guests will be getting a cleverly worded Evite®.

7 How many guests will you invite?

a. At least 200

b. About 100

c. 30 of your closest friends and relatives

8 The most romantic thing your husband could do for you on your wedding day would be to:

a. get teary-eyed when he sees you walk down the aisle.

b. write his own super-sweet vows.

c. sing you a song that he wrote.

9 You and your new husband can travel anywhere in the world for your honeymoon. Where do you choose?

a. Hawaii

b. Italy

c. South Africa

HAWAII

Answers

Mostly A's
Fitting Fairytale

You want to look and feel like a princess on your wedding day, complete with a ball gown and traditional veil. A large affair with tons of friends and family to wish you well, your big day will rival any celebrity bash you've ever seen on TV!

Mostly B's
Simple and Sweet

A huge and formal to-do is not your style. It is more important to you to have your loved ones there with you when you tie the knot in an intimate setting. You envision your wedding like an elegant garden party full of joy, laughter, and celebration.

Mostly C's
Unique Union

Your wedding will be completely unconventional—if you don't end up eloping first! You hate doing things by the book and want your wedding to reflect that. It'll be a carefree day that suits you and your new husband perfectly.

DIY or CEO?

Hands-on helper or perfect planner? How do you make things happen?

1 You're in the waiting room at the doctor's office. On the table are a stack of magazines, a book of puzzles, and some blank paper and pencils. Which do you pick up?

a. Blank paper and pencils

b. Magazines

c. Book of puzzles

2 You find a bunch of old hair ribbons in your drawer. What do you do with them?

a. Make a braided belt

b. Put them back where you found them. You'll find a use for them someday.

c. Keep a few to wear and toss the rest

3 You want to help out with an upcoming school dance. You choose to be responsible for:

a. turning the gym into an underwater extravaganza—to match the theme of the dance.

b. handing out fliers to students, putting a listing in the school paper, and spreading the word about the tickets.

c. hiring the DJ and figuring out how much money will be left over for food and decorations.

4 You see a beautiful beaded bracelet at the mall. After eyeing it for several minutes, you:

a. put it back. You can totally make something similar—and maybe even better—yourself.

b. buy it. It'll look really cute with your new shirt.

c. ask the salesperson if you can have a discount for buying two (in different colors, of course!). Your best friend's birthday is coming up and she would love one, too.

5 If you had your choice in art class, which project would you pick?

a. Sculpting with clay

b. Creating a collage

c. Black-and-white photography

6 It's your parents' anniversary. For a gift, you:

a. make them a photo collage.

b. secretly invite your whole family over for a surprise party.

c. offer to watch your little brothers while they go out to dinner.

7 Hanging on the walls of your bedroom are:

a. framed photos of you and all of your friends.

b. posters of your favorite bands and celebrities.

c. pictures of sunsets that you bought on a family vacation last year.

8 You have to participate in the next issue of the school newspaper. The ideal job for you is:

a. to contribute a poem or drawing to the arts and entertainment section.

b. convincing a few neighborhood stores to take out advertisements.

c. on the editorial page. You'd be happy to tell the readers what you think about the new year-round-school proposal!

ANSWERS

Mostly A's
DIY DESIGNER

You love to make things and often can create cool pieces of art out of virtually nothing. You are not afraid to get messy while creating things. With your talent for translating the cool pictures you envision onto the page or the canvas, you'd make a great photo editor, graphic designer, or potter someday.

Mostly B's
HUNTER AND GATHERER

You're great at bringing people together and getting them excited about a cause—whether it's a worthy charity or your favorite band's new CD release. You love mining the mall for trends and know how to put together clever fashion combinations. You may have a career as an event planner or publicist ahead of you.

Mostly C's
SHARP STUDY

Whether it is the morning news, the story line of your favorite TV show, or your friend's chances with her crush, you love to analyze everything. You are responsible and have a knack for putting together a million details to form a well-thought-out idea or plan. With your abilities, you'd make a great lawyer or psychologist.

Can You Handle It?

Can you roll with whatever life hands you? Or are you forever freaking out?

1 You're on a class camping trip, and it never occurred to you that you'd actually have to sleep in a tent—with four of your classmates. You:

  a. start setting up your site. It's a good thing you brought a warm sleeping bag!

  b. use your cell phone to find out where the nearest hotel is and then beg your teacher to take you there. You and nature don't mix.

  c. are totally grossed out when a worm crawls on you, but try not to think about it. Worms don't carry diseases, do they?

2 You failed two math tests in a row. To save your grade, you need to do an hour of algebra practice a night. You:

  a. think about dropping out of school and working at your local coffee shop—anything would be better than this!

  b. complain about your situation to anyone who will listen but still hit the books every night.

  c. are just thankful for the chance to bring up your grade, no matter what you have to do.

3 It rained last night, and on your walk to school a bus speeds by and splatters your new white tank top with mud. You:

  a. harass all of your friends until someone coughs up an extra shirt.

  b. throw a tantrum. This is unbelievable! You can't go to school like this!

  c. wash the dirt off your skin and wear your new "splattered chic" shirt without shame. A little dirt never hurt anyone, right?

4 One of the popular girls starts spreading nasty rumors about you, and now everyone's been pointing and whispering about you all day. You:

  a. confront that loudmouth. You have to quash this before it ruins your rep.

  b. spread a nasty rumor about her in return. Two can play that game.

  c. let it blow over. Next week, she'll pick on someone else, and all will be forgotten.

5 You have a crush on one of your older brother's friends, and that meddling snoop told him! Next time your crush visits, you:

  a. try not to look him in the eye.

  b. treat him the same way you always have and hope your face isn't turning bright red.

  c. hide in your room until he leaves. Oh, the embarrassment.

6 You tried out for the soccer, softball, and volleyball teams this year—and didn't make any of them. You:

a. are upset for a few days, but then decide to refocus your energies. Maybe cheerleading?

b. take it as a sign that you're not meant to be an athlete and give the school newspaper a try.

c. refuse to try out for another sport ever again. You just can't handle the rejection.

7 Your best friend is having a huge party—and you're grounded for arguing with your mom. You:

a. are devastated. If you miss this party, you'll be totally out of the loop.

b. apologize and ask your parents to compromise: If they let you go to the party, they can add an extra week to your punishment.

c. make your friend promise to tell you everything that happens.

8 You go for a swim at the town pool. As you dive into the water, you feel your bikini top fall off. What do you do?

a. Slowly make your way over to the side of the pool where you carefully retie it. Phew, that was close!

b. Cover your chest with your arms and scream for your sister to help you.

c. Stay under water until you almost pass out. You'd rather die than be seen like this.

Answers

1 a=3 b=1 c=2
2 a=1 b=2 c=3
3 a=2 b=1 c=3
4 a=2 b=1 c=3
5 a=2 b=3 c=1
6 a=2 b=3 c=1
7 a=1 b=2 c=3
8 a=3 b=2 c=1

20–24 points
Bring It On

How do you do it? Staying cool and calm in tough situations is a precious gift! Somehow you know that you're always going to pull through, and that keeps you from blowing things out of proportion. Your level head is an inspiration to your friends.

14–19 points
Partially Panicky

When something goes wrong, your immediate reaction is to freak out. But after a few minutes of meltdown, you realize that getting hysterical isn't going to help matters. Once you calm down, you are a totally helpful problem solver.

8–13 points
Drama Queen

Even the slightest trouble becomes a huge deal where you're concerned. You often get yourself worked up over nothing. Life is hard enough when you aren't prone to overreacting. Try taking ten deep breaths whenever the going gets tough.

In a World with NO SCHOOL...

How would you spend your days?

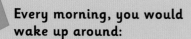

1. Every morning, you would wake up around:

a. 9 a.m. Not too early, not too late.

b. sunrise. You love the early morning.

c. noon. You're not getting up if you don't have to.

2. For breakfast, you'd:

a. try out the new French toast recipe you found yesterday.

b. have cereal and fruit. You want to stay healthy.

c. grab a great big slice of chocolate cake.

3. You'd spend most of the morning:

a. learning to knit or going for a hike.

b. writing in your blog or trying your hand at a screenplay.

c. watching TV.

4. You'd definitely make sure to read:

a. all the books by your favorite author.

b. the daily newspaper.

c. *US Weekly* and *Star* magazines.

5. It's a warm sunny day. What do you do?

a. Go for a nice long run in the morning, then spend the afternoon painting the flowers in your mom's garden

b. Have a picnic with a few friends who might be interested in starting some sort of business together

c. Pile on the sunscreen and settle down on the floating raft in your pool

6. Since you don't have any homework to contend with, your mom puts you in charge of the yard. What do you do with it?

a. Plant a garden complete with tomatoes, cucumbers, peppers, and zucchini. You will have a new hobby—and the freshest salads in the neighborhood!

b. Put up a net so that you, your friends, and your family can play volleyball and badminton games together

c. Mow the grass once every month and a half when it starts to look like you live in a jungle

7 How much time would you spend on the computer?

a. Lots. You'll check out cutting-edge music, write in your blog, look up cool facts, and meet new people.

b. Just enough to keep up with your emails and IM your friends about getting together

c. Very little—you prefer to watch TV

8 With more time at home, you decide to catch up on your movie watching. What kind of flicks do you pick?

a. A mixture. You'll make sure to see all the movies your friends talk about, but also check out Oscar-winners and some classic films that your parents insist are must-see movies.

b. As long as it's not too serious, you'll watch it! Since you are on an extended vacation, you grab romances, goofy comedies, and blockbusters first.

c. You aren't too picky. You will watch whatever is on TV. Luckily, thanks to your love of TV, you have lots and lots of channels to choose from.

9 You'd never:

a. let yourself become lazy.

b. spend your day cooped up inside.

c. wake up to an alarm clock again.

ANSWERS

Mostly A's
BUILD A BETTER YOU

You like to relax, but you don't want to become too lazy, so you'd set boundaries and create goals for improving yourself. Whether it is learning to count to ten in several languages or teaching yourself to decorate handbags, you would keep giving your brain a good workout.

Mostly B's
ENTERPRISING AND ENERGETIC

You'd go crazy just sitting around. If you aren't stuck in school, you'll find new ways to keep yourself busy. Maybe you could set up a greeting-card business, write columns for the local paper, shampoo hair at a nearby salon, or help your neighbors out around the house?

Mostly C's
RELAXATION NATION

You hate the rules and rigidity of school, so now you'll do whatever you want. Sleep late, eat junk food, veg out in front of the television, and play all the video games you want—all the stuff that's hard to do when you spend eight hours a day in a classroom. From now on, it's all about fun!

If You Were in the **olympics...**

In which sport would you go for the gold?

1 **When studying for a test, you like to:**

  a. work in a group, with everyone helping one another to do well.

  b. make flash cards and then, with a friend, take turns quizzing each another on the material.

  c. wait until the last minute and then cram everything into your brain all at once.

  d. set aside an hour each day to reread your notes so that you memorize the information little by little.

2 **You like to watch sports that:**

  a. are fast-paced, with a lot of action happening all of the time.

  b. involve races, with one person reaching the finish line before another.

  c. are extreme and maybe a little dangerous.

  d. require style, poise, and performing in front of a crowd.

3 **You're at a class picnic, and there are tons of activities going on. You head straight for:**

  a. the basketball court. If there is a game going on, you want in!

  b. the swimming pool. It sure is hot out!

  c. the trampoline. You want to practice your double backflip.

  d. the dance floor. The DJ's playing your favorite song.

4 **You hate being:**

  a. confined to small spaces.

  b. far away from water.

  c. bored.

  d. misunderstood.

5 Your favorite season is:

a. fall.
b. summer.
c. winter.
d. spring.

7 Sometimes you wish you would:

a. relax a little.
b. trust people more easily.
c. think before you act.
d. have more free time.

6 Your friends might describe you as:

a. energetic.
b. quiet.
c. fearless.
d. graceful.

8 The animal you identify with most is:

a. a wolf.
b. a dolphin.
c. a leopard.
d. a swan.

Answers

Mostly A's
Soccer Fiend

You thrive on the spirit and camaraderie that comes with competing as a group, so winning by yourself is just not the ideal. You're a great team player with boundless energy, so an action-packed soccer game would be perfect for you.

Mostly B's
Waterbaby

Your competitive streak is perfect for swim meets where you can push yourself to new feats. You may be a bit shy and value your alone time, but you definitely have the discipline and dedication it takes to become a champion swimmer.

Mostly C's
Ski Sloper

Heights certainly don't bother you, and speed is a breeze! You're a thrill seeker and love a good adrenaline rush. Nothing scares you—not even standing atop a 200-foot mountain! Something extreme like snowboarding is your way forward.

Mostly D's
Ice Princess

You live for applause and love to perform in front of a crowd. For you, a sport needs artistry as well as athleticism. You also have incredible strength, flexibility, and poise—everything you need to be an amazing skater.

What Does Your Bag Say about You?

See what your carryall reveals about your personality.

1 Which of the following bags would you choose for an everyday bag?

a. An oversized purple tote
b. A dark green knapsack
c. A small designer handbag

2 Inside your bag you keep:

a. everything you can think of. It's practically overflowing.
b. just the essentials: cell phone, book, money, lip gloss, gum, and hairbrush.
c. as little as possible. Heavy bags hurt your shoulder.

3 The outside of your bag:

a. has a hole in the side pocket from excessive use.
b. is covered with doodles and drawings that you made when you were bored.
c. is as perfect as the day you got it. You don't want to ruin it.

4 When you're at school, you:

a. carry your bag with you because it doesn't fit in your locker.
b. stash it in your locker unless you really need it.
c. never let it out of your sight. It completes your outfit.

5 If you lost your bag, you'd be most upset because:

a. it has your entire life in it.
b. you've had it since fourth grade, and it has sentimental value.
c. it cost three months' allowance.

Answers

Mostly A's
Busy Bee

You juggle tons of activities, so you need a big bag to carry all of your stuff. But when you cram everything into one tote, you can never find what you're looking for. Empty out your bag and only put back what you absolutely need—like two hair clips instead of ten.

Mostly B's
Totally Traditional

Your backpack isn't only an accessory. It's a reflection of who you are. You're a deep, caring soul who values sentimentality. Yes, your bag transports your daily needs, but it also tells the story of you: what you like and dislike, the hobbies and friends you enjoy, and how you feel.

Mostly C's
Dashing Diva

You're sassy and stylish and always take note of the designer handbags in the fashion mags. Whether this is your first "it" bag or your fiftieth, you treat them all with the utmost care. Someday you hope to pass down your love of purses and your fashion flair to your own daughter.

SOCCER

Are You a **TRIVIA** Buff?

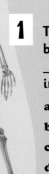

1 The human body has _____ bones in it.

a. 420

b. 53

c. 206

d. 1,347

2 Who was the 16th president of the United States?

a. John F. Kennedy

b. Andrew Jackson

c. Abraham Lincoln

d. Dwight Eisenhower

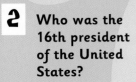

3 If you have anemophobia, you are afraid of:

a. school.

b. air.

c. bugs.

d. frogs.

4 The first woman doctor was:

a. Elizabeth Blackwell.

b. Elizabeth Cady Stanton.

c. Elizabeth Ann Seton.

d. Elizabeth Barrett Browning.

5 What are female turkeys called?

a. Birdies

b. Roosters

c. Chickadees

d. Hens

6 What is the longest river in the world?

a. Amazon

b. Nile

c. Mississippi

d. Ganges

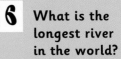

7 Which one of these is not a nut?

a. Walnut

b. Peanut

c. Almond

d. Hazelnut

ANSWERS

1 c. We're born with as many as 300 bones, but some fuse together as we grow.

2 c. Abraham Lincoln was the 16th president and was in the White House during the Civil War.

3 b. Anemophobics are afraid of air and wind.

4 a. Elizabeth Blackwell received her medical degree in 1849, making her the first woman ever to do so.

5 d. Female turkeys are known as hens.

6 b. The Nile, located in Africa, is more than 4,100 miles long.

7 b. A peanut is actually a legume like a soybean or a lentil.

YOUR SCORE

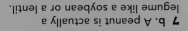

6–7 correct

TRIVIA MANIAC

Where've you been hiding all of that extra knowledge? Quick, go challenge your siblings to a game of Trivial Pursuit®!

3–5 correct

WIN SOME, LOSE SOME

You know a lot of fun facts, but you can always learn more. Whenever you hear a neat bit of trivia, write it down—it helps you to remember.

0–2 correct

NEED A REFRESHER

Get out that encyclopedia, pick a subject, and get to it. Reading is the best way to pick up cool facts. Soon you'll be a whiz.

Do You Blush Too Much?

What does it take to totally embarrass you?

START

In gym class, the boy you like finally said more than two words to you, and they were: "Hey, you have spinach in your teeth." You:

say, "Guess we're even because you've got a booger in your nose."

mumble "Thanks" and beat it back over to where your friends are standing.

stare at him, stunned. This must be what it feels like to die.

Your mom has a habit of showing your naked baby pictures to every friend you bring to the house. You:

suffer in silence. In twenty years this'll be funny.

run and hide until the torture is over.

You found a bunch of cute clothes at the mall, but when you go to try them on, you see that none of the fitting rooms have doors. You:

start trying the clothes on. This top is going to look so cute with your new jean skirt!

reluctantly go in but ask your mom to stand guard and shield you.

put everything back and walk out. You're not getting naked in front of strangers!

At your dance recital, you wipe out in the middle of your solo. You:

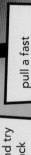

pull a fast sit spin. The audience will never know you weren't supposed to land on your butt.

furiously bite your lip and try to hold back the tears.

You're hanging out at home with a friend when your brother walks into the room, loudly farts, and then walks out. You:

You walk in on your dad and mom kissing. You:

You are at a fancy restaurant with a friend's family, and you mispronounce the name of a dish. When the waiter corrects you, you:

- clear your throat, to let them know you're in the room. You think it's sweet that they're still so in love.

- loudly yell, "Ewwl" until they quit acting like lovebirds.

You and your friends are climbing a tree. On the way down, a branch snags the back of your pants leaving a big hole. You:

- scream, sit down, and refuse to get up until someone brings you a blanket for cover.

- wrap a sweater around your waist and calmly go home to change.

- laugh along with him and are glad to know how to say it in the future.

- cringe and hope no one was paying attention.

- are sure you'll never be invited out again. You sounded like such a moron.

- remark that your brother must have been adopted, because clearly he was raised by wolves.

At dinner with your family, your mom blurts out that you should start wearing a bra. You:

- tell her you want a hot pink one like your best friend has. Your whole family helps with the laundry, so it's not like your new skivvies would be a secret for long anyway.

- say, "Mom, do we really need to talk about this now?!" and change the subject.

You walk out of the locker room at school not realizing that the back of your skirt is tucked into your underwear. You:

- assume no one noticed—since you would've heard the laughter. And thank goodness you had cute undies on!

- seriously think about flinging your peas at her.

- head straight to the nurse's office and fake sick so you can go home. How will you ever show your face again?

- are mortified. What is wrong with your family?

Cool Cucumber

Nothing bothers you—spinach in your teeth, tripping in the hallways, not even walking in on your dad in the loo. You're a very open person and realize that everyone has embarrassing moments. You can even share yours, which makes others feel better, too.

Bit of a Blusher

You are pretty down-to-earth, but sometimes you just can't help feeling uncomfortable—like when your family does something totally horrifying or you mess up in public. That's completely normal. Even the coolest people feel self-conscious sometimes.

Burning Up

Even the slightest discomfort makes your face fire-engine red. But remember, mortifying things happen to everyone. Next time you feel your cheeks heating up, try laughing off whatever's bothering you. At least your face will be red for a fun reason!

Do You Like Him For the RIGHT REASONS?

What is it about your crush that makes you go ga-ga?

1 **What is the first thing you noticed about him?**

a. His super-dreamy eyes

b. His knack for getting into trouble in math class

c. His fun-loving laugh

2 **Last weekend, you took your dog on a long walk in the park. He was there too. What was he doing?**

a. Just hanging out

b. Playing baseball

c. Tossing a ball around with his little brother

3 **You are making masks in art class and he needs to use the glue gun after you. While you are making your finishing touches, he:**

a. sticks around and helps hold your project in place while you apply the glue.

b. grabs the gun when you aren't looking and takes it back to his desk even though you aren't done.

c. asks you to shout for him when you are done.

4 **When he's around a group of girls, he usually:**

a. makes fun of them.

b. flirts up a storm.

c. doesn't say much.

5 You have to attend a school assembly. By the time you get there, there's only one seat left—next to him, you:

a. feel completely comfortable sitting down next to him.

b. are nervous. You hope you'll get to talk to him a little bit.

c. panic and ask everyone to move down a seat so you can sit on the end of the row.

6 When you interact with him, you:

a. are frustrated that he's always clowning around.

b. are exhilarated. He's so much fun.

c. feel anxious. Is there any way he'd actually like you?

7 You can't help but grin when you:

a. daydream about him asking you to a dance—or even talking to you at all.

b. remember him having to read a poem out loud in English class.

c. think of that one time when he walked you home.

8 If you started going out with your crush, how much time would you expect to spend with him?

a. As much as possible. He doesn't need to spend time with any other girls as long as he has you.

b. A few hours a week outside of school—you both have after-school activities, but would make time to hang out or talk on the phone.

c. None outside of school and the occasional dance.

ANSWERS

1 a=2 b=3 c=1
2 a=3 b=2 c=1
3 a=1 b=3 c=2
4 a=3 b=2 c=1
5 a=1 b=2 c=3
6 a=3 b=1 c=2
7 a=3 b=2 c=1
8 a=3 b=1 c=2

7–11 points
PERFECT PICK

This guy's a total sweetie and would make a great boyfriend. He's thoughtful, caring, and shares many of the same interests as you. Even better than that, you feel good around him, and that is one of the keys to finding Mr. Right.

12–16 points
MAYBE, BABY

He might not be totally sure you exist, but he does sound like a cool character and someone worth getting to know better. It also sounds like you are still a little bit nervous around him, so take your time. There's no need to rush things.

17–21 points
UNLIKELY OPTION

This guy sounds like someone you should run from not towards! He's trouble and is way too immature to even think about being nice to a girl. Plus, going after the bad boy type only sets you up for trouble later.

Are You a High-Maintenance Friend?

Are you difficult to deal with? Or a laid-back lady?

1 You made plans to hang out with a friend. She wants to go to the mall, but you'd rather see a movie. You:

   a. tell her that you'll be at the theater and she's welcome to join you.

   b. suggest that you go shopping first, then take in a film.

   c. agree to go to the mall. You can always see a movie some other time.

2 Your best friend forgot to call you on your birthday. When she finally phones you—two days later—to apologize, you:

   a. tell her not to sweat it. You'll have another birthday next year.

   b. let her know that you're really hurt but will get over it. You'd better be getting one heck of a present!

   c. refuse to take her calls. She's dead to you now. How rude!

3 You're a vegetarian, but a friend's family has invited you to dinner— at a steakhouse. When the menu comes and the meat-free options are dreary at best, you:

   a. slide the bread basket closer to you and plan on ordering a huge dessert.

   b. start making whimpering noises and remind them how cows are slaughtered. They should pay more attention before taking someone out to dinner!

   c. whisper to the waiter that you don't eat animals and hope he brings you something edible.

4 You hate reality television, but your friends are addicted. When they talk about the plotlines of their favorite shows, you:

   a. suffer in silence.

   b. get up in a huff and walk away. They are so annoying.

   c. don't understand how they care so much about the lives of strangers.

5 You texted your friend ten minutes ago, and she hasn't replied yet. You:

   a. text her again. And then again. What could she be doing that's so important?

   b. wait twenty minutes, then send her another message.

   c. don't worry about it. She's really busy and will get back to you when she can.

6 You're hanging out at a friend's house and have a major craving for ice cream. Unfortunately, the freezer's bare. You:

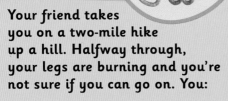

a. ask her if she's up for taking a walk to the corner store to get some. She can choose the flavor.

b. demand that her older brother go on an ice cream run. Seriously, he doesn't have anything better to do.

c. spot a bag of pretzels in the cupboard and snack on those instead.

7 Your friend takes you on a two-mile hike up a hill. Halfway through, your legs are burning and you're not sure if you can go on. You:

a. plop down on the nearest tree trunk and refuse to move. She dragged you up here, now it's her job to get you down.

b. stick it out. You should be fine, if only you could catch your breath.

c. suggest that you take a break before continuing on. You could use it.

8 How important is it that your friends have a lot in common with you?

a. Very important. You can't relate to people who don't think in exactly the same way you do.

b. Somewhat important. It's easier to be close to people who like to do the same things as you.

c. Not important. You just want as many friends as possible.

9 Your friend Liz's parents are having a barbecue this weekend because some family friends are visiting from out of town. Liz does not invite you over to meet her old childhood buds. How do you feel?

a. Not bothered at all. It is up to her and her family to decide on a guest list. If it was appropriate to invite you, they would have.

b. A little bit sad. You would love to meet her old friends. They must know really silly stories from when she was younger.

c. Extremely hurt. You would never have a barbecue without inviting her.

Answers

1 a=3 b=2 c=1
2 a=1 b=2 c=3
3 a=2 b=3 c=1
4 a=1 b=3 c=2
5 a=3 b=2 c=1
6 a=2 b=3 c=1
7 a=3 b=1 c=2
8 a=3 b=2 c=1
9 a=1 b=2 c=3

One Picky Pal
22–27 points
You require tons of attention, and if your friends don't do exactly what you want, you get mad at them. Chill out! Friendship is a two-way street. You need to embrace other people's opinions and ideas if you ever expect them to respect yours.

Cooperative Cohort
16–21 points
You understand that people's schedules don't always line up and sometimes you have to be patient. At times, you need to have it your way, but you are aware that the spotlight won't always be on you. Life would be boring if everyone always agreed with you.

Low-Key Lass
9–15 points
You are one easy-going gal! You don't get miffed if your friends don't call back immediately or if a situation doesn't go your way. While your easygoing nature is appreciated, don't be afraid to speak up if you feel like someone is taking you for granted.

What's Your Dream Car?

That driver's license is almost within reach.
What will your ride look like?

1 **Without a doubt, your car must:**

a. look hot.

b. be big enough to cart around all of your friends.

c. have a lot of cutting-edge features.

d. be good for the environment.

2 **You'd be happy if your car also came with:**

a. leather seats.

b. a navigation system.

c. amazing speakers.

d. a bike rack.

3 **You want the color of your car to be:**

a. silver.

b. red.

c. black.

d. green.

4 **How much time will you spend in your vehicle?**

a. Plenty—you want to see and be seen in your sleek wheels.

b. Lots—your automobile will be the ultimate for road trips!

c. No more than you need to. Plus, you'd prefer someone else to run the errands for you.

d. Not much. It will be helpful for carrying things or taking you places that you can't get to on foot or on your bike.

5 **You will not be OK with:**

a. anyone eating or drinking in the car.

b. people who won't wear their seatbelts.

c. having to pump your own gas. You would prefer to have a driver!

d. your friends leaving their garbage in your car.

Answers

Mostly A's
Trendmobile
Whatever the auto of-the-moment is, you have to have it. You like attractive, sporty cars like Ferraris or BMWs that will make people stop and stare. You will take wonderful care of all the cars you own throughout your life.

Mostly B's
Roomy Ride
It's no fun driving your dream car if your friends can't enjoy it with you. While you drive your SUV, they can kick back and watch TV or keep the tunes coming on your super-cool stereo. You would love a Range Rover or Cadillac Escalade.

Mostly C's
Luxury Wheels
You're all about the finer things in life, and your car's no exception. You want your top-of-the-line car to come fully loaded with every available gadget. If not a limo with a driver, then a Mercedes or Lexus would please your inner diva.

Mostly D's
Eco-Car
You definitely want a cool car, but you know that the pollution caused by automobile exhaust is a huge problem. You'd never drive a gas-guzzler, so you'll keep the environment in mind. A compact hybrid car's the one for you.

What's Your Dream Date?

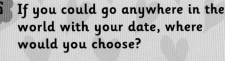

What would you do on a perfect night out?

1 When your date shows up at your door, you see he's carrying something. Which of these would be the coolest?

a. An autographed copy of your favorite CD that he found on eBay

b. Two hockey sticks, in case you want to play

c. Two dozen red roses—he says you deserve beautiful things

d. A copy of his favorite book—he thought you might like it

2 Your first stop is:

a. a picnic lunch at the park.

b. a football game.

c. a candlelit dinner.

d. an independent film at your local coffeehouse.

3 On the date, you mainly talk about:

a. your lives, your families, and where you grew up.

b. all of the cool places you've both been.

c. how much he likes you.

d. books, movies, and what's going on in the world.

4 If you were to see a movie on your date, you would choose:

a. the big drama out this season—you hear it'll be up for an Oscar!

b. an action-packed flick, like the one about surfers in Hawaii—it looks wild!

c. something scary so you'd have an excuse to hold hands.

d. the controversial environmental documentary that everyone is talking about.

5 If you could go anywhere in the world with your date, where would you choose?

a. His childhood hometown—he has told you so many stories that you would love to see it in person

b. To the final game of the World Series—you could cheer together in the front row

c. The Eiffel Tower—he could kiss you under the stars, looking out over Paris

d. A political rally in Washington —together, you could make a difference in the world

Answers

Mostly A's
Romantic Rendezvous

You are impressed by a guy who listens to you and remembers what you like. You don't need expensive gifts and pricey meals. You just want to get to know each other, so leisurely picnics, long walks, and hours on the phone are up your alley.

Mostly B's
Outdoor Outings

You love to be outdoors tackling new and different activities. To stand out in a crowd, a guy needs to plan adventures for you. Biking, beach volleyball, white-water rafting, hiking in the woods, and exploring are exciting dates for you and your guy.

Mostly C's
Fancy Feasts

To really win your heart, a guy needs to wine and dine you, like they do in old movies. You expect flowers, chocolates, dinners, show tickets, tons of compliments, and for him to profess his undying love. When you think of kissing him goodnight, you want to see stars.

Mostly D's
Debate and Date

You're a huge reader and environmentalist who relates to guys who share your interest in the world around you. If you're having a good discussion about books, politics, or the future, it doesn't matter if you're relaxing under a tree or at a five-star restaurant.

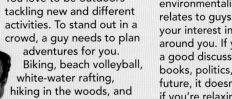

How GREEN Are You?

What is your environmental IQ? See how you score.

1 You live in walking distance of school. How do you get there?
- **a.** You take the bus.
- **b.** You walk.
- **c.** You get your mom to drive you.

2 You're brushing your teeth before bed. Do you leave the water running?
- **a.** No
- **b.** Yes
- **c.** Sometimes, although you try to remember to turn it off

3 You're at the park and notice a few soda cans littering the ground. You:
- **a.** walk them to the recycling bin even though it is far away.
- **b.** toss them into the nearby trash can.
- **c.** leave them on the ground.

4 In order to fall asleep, you need to watch TV before bed. Who turns it off?
- **a.** You set a timer to turn it off at midnight.
- **b.** You do, as soon as you feel yourself getting drowsy.
- **c.** Your mom probably does. You're not really sure—you are snoozing!

5 When you clean your room, what do you do with the old toys and clothes you've outgrown?
- **a.** Donate them to a local charity
- **b.** Drop them off at the dump
- **c.** Put them in the attic. Maybe someone else in the family will need them someday.

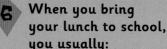

6 When you bring your lunch to school, you usually:
- **a.** grab one of the bags your parents have saved from shopping or going to the grocery store.
- **b.** pack your snacks in a reusable canvas bag that helps keep your food cool.
- **c.** use a brown paper bag each day.

7 How many hours a day is your computer usually on?

a. 24/7

b. Twelve, although you do put it to sleep to conserve energy

c. Three or four—but only when you're using it

8 Have you ever volunteered at a local park or environmental organization?

a. No

b. Yes

c. Not yet, but you plan to soon

9 Your parents are redoing your backyard. You encourage them to:

a. install a Jacuzzi so you can relax in style.

b. build a huge deck so you can lie out and get a tan.

c. plant a row of trees—they produce oxygen and help make the air cleaner.

10 You finish up your plastic water bottle and look around for somewhere to throw it away. You see a few trash cans, but no recycling bins nearby. What do you?

a. Just toss it

b. Put it in your backpack so you can recycle it when you get home

c. Refill the bottle at the water fountain. You can use it a few more times before recycling it.

ANSWERS

1	a=2	b=3	c=1
2	a=3	b=1	c=2
3	a=3	b=2	c=1
4	a=2	b=3	c=1
5	a=3	b=1	c=2
6	a=2	b=3	c=1
7	a=1	b=2	c=3
8	a=1	b=3	c=2
9	a=2	b=1	c=3
10	a=1	b=2	c=3

24–30 points

EARTH ANGEL

You're doing a ton of great work to save the planet and are really conscious of the effect your habits have on your surroundings. Now if only you could get your friends to do the same! Make sure to spread the word. Keep up the great work!

17–23 points

A FOR EFFORT

You may care about the Earth and want to do your part, but sometimes you forget to turn off lights or conserve water. Maybe you should go online and look for other ways you can make a difference. The more you know, the more attention you'll pay to your routines.

10–15 points

LIVING UNDER A ROCK

Are you even aware that the environment is in danger? Next time you're tempted to litter or leave on all the lights in your house, think about how bad that will be for the planet. You want your children to inherit a nice, clean, safe place, don't you?

How FEARLESS Are You?

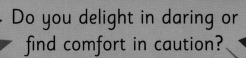

Do you delight in daring or find comfort in caution?

1 You're watching television on the couch when a spider crawls across your leg. You:

a. flick it onto the floor. It's okay for spiders to be inside because they kill other bugs.

b. squash it dead.

c. start screaming bloody murder for your mom to get it off you.

2 You're at an amusement park with some friends and they all want to ride the "Vomit Comet," a rollercoaster with ten upside down loops. You:

a. say that you'll sit out their first time, but maybe try it later.

b. break into a run as soon as you catch a glimpse of the ride. You hope you can ride in the first car!

c. agree to go on—as long as you are surrounded by your best friends. You can't guarantee that you won't barf afterwards…

3 Which of the following is the craziest height you hope to experience?

a. Walking to the top of the Statue of Liberty

b. Having lunch on a friend's second-floor balcony

c. Sky-diving

4 There's a haunted house in your neighborhood and one of your friends dares you to spend two hours inside. You:

a. agree, but make her come with you. You're not doing that alone.

b. are totally up for it. There's no such thing as a haunted house and you're going to prove it. Maybe you can scare her on your way out!

c. tell her you really don't want to die from a heart attack before you're twenty.

5 Your mom enrolls you in a gymnastics class. When it's time to get up on the balance beam, you:

a. leap right up there. You wonder if they'll let you try a cartwheel so soon.

b. fake a cramp and sit this one out.

c. slowly practice walking on such a narrow surface. You're sure you'll get the hang of it soon.

6 Your teacher tells your class that each one of you will have to give a ten-minute oral presentation next week. You:

a. calculate how badly an F will affect your grade, because there's no way you're standing up there in front of everyone.

b. start practicing in front of the mirror. You don't want to look as nervous as you feel.

c. ask if you can go first. You get a rush in front of an audience.

7 Your friend's dad rented a trampoline for her birthday party. As you watch her brother jumping and flipping, you:

a. beg him to stop. Doesn't he know how dangerous those things are?

b. hope he gets off soon. You have some cool moves you want to show off too.

c. wish you could move that gracefully.

8 You're on vacation at a lake house and just as you are about to dive in, you see something move in the lake. You:

a. run inside. Maybe swimming isn't such a good idea after all.

b. grab a net and check it out. Maybe it was just a log?

c. ask your brother to help you investigate what caused the mysterious movement.

9 You walk into gym class before the teacher one day and see a group of kids picking on a younger student. What do you do?

a. You don't get involved. You don't want them picking on you either.

b. You march over there, demand to know what it going on, and tell them to pick on people their own size

c. Go out to the hallway to see if you can flag down a teacher

10 Your parents are planning a tropical family vacation. They mention that you can go swimming in 'shark alley' if you want. When they ask if you are interested, you say:

a. "Are you crazy? There are sharks in there?!"

b. "Sure, I'll go. As long as we're all there together." If they are offering packaged trips, it must be safe.

c. "I'm so there! Can we buy underwater disposable cameras so we can get pictures with the sharks? I wouldn't miss it for the world."

ANSWERS

1	a=3	b=2 c=1
2	a=2	b=3 c=1
3	a=2	b=1 c=3
4	a=2	b=3 c=1
5	a=3	b=1 c=2
6	a=1	b=2 c=3
7	a=1	b=3 c=2
8	a=1	b=3 c=2
9	a=2	b=3 c=1
10	a=1	b=2 c=3

20–24 points
HAVE NO FEAR
You'll try anything once. And you'd rather die than admit to being afraid of something. Just don't mistake fearlessness for recklessness. You don't want to get injured just to prove a point.

14–19 points
DISCERNING DAREDEVIL
You've got a healthy amount of apprehension. While you like to challenge yourself and try new things, you also know when you're pushing the limit. You trust your gut to guide you.

8–13 points
RARE RISKTAKER
You don't like to take risks and rarely accept dares. But if you let yourself ride a roller coaster or watch a scary movie, you might like the adrenaline rush!

Are You a TOMBOY?

Baseball or debutante ball? Which is more your style?

START

Your usual uniform is:

a cute skirt and matching headband. You have so much fun coordinating your ensembles.

T-shirts, jeans, and sneakers. You don't like to spend a lot of time agonizing about what to wear.

a mix of cargo pants, flip flops, and tanks.

When you have nothing to do on a Saturday afternoon, you like to:

go to the mall. Whether you are trying on clothes or just checking out cool stuff, you are happy to shop 'till you drop!

ride your bike around the neighborhood. You are always up for an adventure.

If you consider all of the friends you've had in your life, you would say you get along best with:

girls.

well...everybody. Your group of friends has both guys and girls.

guys.

Your mom wishes you would:

If you had to pick between the two, which sport would you rather watch?

Football—you really get into the strategy and the rivalries

Figure skating—the music and moves are so graceful

After school, you'd much rather:

This is a quiz flowchart. Start at the top and follow the arrows.

Your parents make you do a lot of chores to earn your allowance. Your favorite is:

- stop stealing her makeup.
- wear your hair down every once in a while.
- mowing the lawn. You love to be outside.
- cleaning your room. Reorganizing your closet is always fun for you.

You got invited to your cousin's wedding and need to get dressed up. You:

- can't decide which dress to wear. You have so many! Plus, there might be cute boys there.
- wonder if the skirt you wore to the last family wedding still fits you.
- ask your mom if wearing pants is an option.

You find out that a boy you grew up with has a crush on you. You:

- wonder what took him so long to notice you!
- think he's kind of cute, too.
- feel really weird. You built a fort at the playground with him when you were seven!

- veg out in front of the TV.
- play outside with the kids in your neighborhood.

For your birthday, you are more likely to ask for:

- a digital camera.
- the hottest new video game system.

Fully Feminine

You're a total girly girl. You like to be pampered and look pretty. Getting your nails done is your idea of fun; getting sweaty is not. You can't help but check yourself out in the mirror because you care about your appearance and always try to look your best.

Casual Cutie

You can appreciate a cute handbag, but at the same time, you aren't obsessed with how you look. From shopping to exercising to hanging out with your many friends, you have a wide range of interests that both boys and girls are into.

Just One of the Guys

You'd much rather play pickup soccer than play dress up any day. And face it, makeup just isn't your idea of fun. You have way more fun being active than those girls who are worried about getting their hair messed up!

What Does YOUR PALM Say About You?

Each one of the lines on your hands reveals something about your personality. What does your palm say about you?

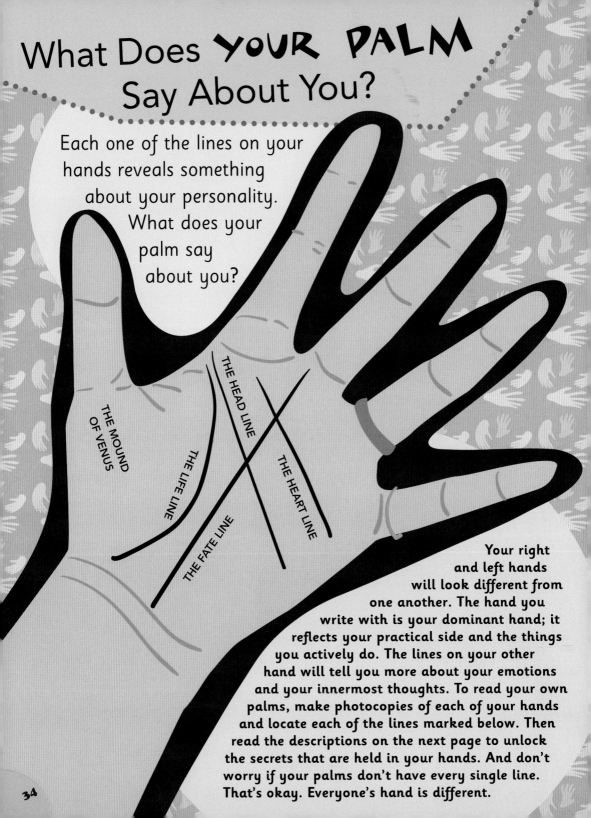

THE HEAD LINE

THE MOUND OF VENUS

THE LIFE LINE

THE FATE LINE

THE HEART LINE

Your right and left hands will look different from one another. The hand you write with is your dominant hand; it reflects your practical side and the things you actively do. The lines on your other hand will tell you more about your emotions and your innermost thoughts. To read your own palms, make photocopies of each of your hands and locate each of the lines marked below. Then read the descriptions on the next page to unlock the secrets that are held in your hands. And don't worry if your palms don't have every single line. That's okay. Everyone's hand is different.

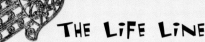

THE LiFE LiNE

Located between the thumb and index finger, the life line is the most important line and can determine what kind of life you will live. Don't panic if you have a short one—this line will not tell you how long you will live. It reveals the quality of the life you lead. People with short, deep life lines can live to be old and grey too! If there is a gap in your life line, that symbolizes a major change you will go through. The life line is curved—if it runs close to the thumb, you may be a tired person. A wide arc indicates that you have great energy. Little lines jutting from your life line may mean that you are a nervous or anxious person.

THE HEAD LiNE

This line represents your intellect and ability to reason. If your head line is located above your life line, you are very independent. If it is starts with your life line, you are cautious and have strong ties to your family. An average head line ends underneath the ring finger. If your head line is longer, you are very good at seeing both sides of an argument, but have trouble making decisions. A shorter line indicates that you don't always think before you act.

THE HEART LiNE

Your heart line symbolizes your emotions and feelings about love. If your heart line begins between your index and middle finger you are both sensitive and practical. If your heart line begins at your index finger, it means you are very emotional and sometimes moody. A straight heart line means that you speak your mind, even if it's hard for others to hear what you have to say.

THE FATE LiNE

This line indicates the effect that outside sources have on your life. A deep fate line suggests that you are a lucky person, while a weak one indicates that you'll have to work hard to get what you want. If your fate line and life line are joined, you may already know what you want to be when you grow up. If your fate line starts at the base of your thumb, you have a lot of love and support in your life. If it starts at the base of the palm, you're destined to be in the public eye. Maybe you'll be a celebrity!

THE MoUND oF VENUS

This is the fleshy part of the palm located underneath the thumb. If you have deep lines there, you are a compassionate and sympathetic person. If your Mound of Venus is full and round, you are a wonderful and kind friend. Someone with a flatter Mound of Venus may be reserved and find it harder to connect with others; or she may be more academic in her pursuits.

What's Your CREATIVE QUOTIENT?

Are you a pictures person
or a word wizard?
How do you express
your imagination?

1 **Its summer vacation!
How are you going
to spend your time?**

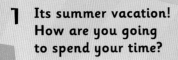

- **a.** Taking a pottery class
- **b.** Going to a rock music camp
- **c.** Writing in your journal
- **d.** Making hilarious home movies with your friends

2 **Your best friend's mom is
planning a surprise party
for her. When you find out,
you immediately:**

- **a.** send her suggestions for themed decorations that your friend would absolutely love.
- **b.** start making a party mix on your iPod.
- **c.** jot down an invitation list.
- **d.** plan to photograph the event. You can't wait to see her face when she walks through the door—and the pics will make a perfect gift for her!

3 **Your room is:**

- **a.** a crazy mess with a million half-finished projects all over the floor.
- **b.** not too cluttered. You need space to do the things you like best, like playing the guitar and rocking out to your favorite tunes.
- **c.** welcoming and relaxing. There are plenty of photos in frames and your many notebooks are the only things on the floor.
- **d.** a great place to hang out. You have a TV and tons of DVDs, so there is always something to do at your house.

4 **You are studying mythology in
school. For your class project,
you choose to:**

- **a.** draw a life-sized portrait of Medusa—complete with the snakes coming out of her head!
- **b.** compose a song about who's who in Ancient Greece.
- **c.** write a report about the story of Orpheus going to the underworld to rescue his true love. It's so tragic and romantic.
- **d.** create a website about Hercules and his labors—complete with cool historical paintings and sculptures.

5 You enter a raffle and win $50. What do you spend it on?

- **a.** New paints and canvases
- **b.** Concert tickets
- **c.** A ton of used books and plays
- **d.** A Broadway show

6 You're sitting at a café with a cup of coffee. What else are you doing?

- **a.** Daydreaming
- **b.** Trying to identify the classical music that's playing in the background
- **c.** Reading a book— and eavesdropping on the table behind you
- **d.** People watching

7 On your bedroom walls, you'll see:

- **a.** a cool mosiac you made in art class.
- **b.** posters of your favorite bands.
- **c.** word collages you made from magazine cutouts.
- **d.** pictures of you and your friends.

ANSWERS

Mostly A's
ARTS AND CRAFTS

You're really good with your hands. Whether you are using foam, fabric, clay, or cardboard, you can create wonders. When you see an amazing necklace or cool handmade purse, you can easily imagine how to recreate it at home. You'd be a great seamstress or potter.

Mostly B's
MUSIC MAKER

You dig a good beat and love to set the tunes to match your mood. Just hearing a song can transport you back to a particular moment in time. If you can't make a career out of playing an instrument, you'd make a great talent scout for a record label.

Mostly C's
LANGUAGE LOVER

You're a writer at heart and love to express yourself through poetry, prose, and the great stories you tell. You constantly come up with scenarios and bits of dialogue to incorporate into your next story. It's your dream to be a novelist or journalist when you get older.

Mostly D's
FILM BUFF

You are a totally visual person. When you read a book or hear someone tell a story, you can perfectly picture the way it looks. You try never to be without your camera so you can capture life's best moments. A career as a photographer or film director is in the cards for you.

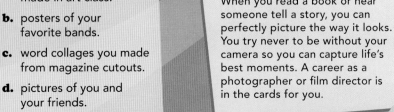

Lights, Camera, or **ACTION**?

On a movie set, will you pull the strings behind the scene or lap up the limelight in front of the camera?

1 Class elections are coming up. You plan on running for:

a. treasurer.

b. school mascot.

c. president.

d. social chair.

2 When a friend is feeling sad, she knows she can always count on you to:

a. let her cry on your shoulder.

b. make her watch horror movies all night—to scare the sadness away.

c. offer suggestions for how to deal with any tough situation.

d. take her shopping to cheer her up.

3 You're going to the movies with a group of friends. Everyone wants to see something different, so you:

a. let your friends battle it out. You don't really mind which movie you see.

b. talk up the fact that the new action flick has a really hot leading man.

c. suggest that you split up into pairs and meet for ice cream afterward. That way, everyone will be happy.

d. tell your crew that you've seen every movie out except one, so if that's not the choice, you'll stay home.

4 Your school has a community-service requirement. What do you volunteer to do?

a. Bake cookies for the library's annual bake sale fund-raiser

b. Join a bike ride-a-thon benefiting cancer research. A forty-mile bike ride won't be that hard, right?

c. Organize a food drive for the less fortunate in your community

d. Participate in a talent show for your local senior center

5 You think your best quality is:

a. your selflessness.

b. your commitment to doing whatever it takes to accomplish a goal.

c. your gift for motivating yourself and others.

d. your ability to speak up for yourself.

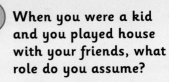 **7** When you were a kid and you played house with your friends, what role do you assume?

a. The wacky aunt

b. The rebellious daughter

c. The understanding mother

d. The glamorous daughter

 6 The school newspaper is looking for people to join its staff. You apply for the position of:

a. style editor. You can spot a trend a mile away.

b. beat reporter. You can't wait to uncover your first big scoop!

c. managing editor. You'll keep things running smoothly.

d. features editor. You have a talent for spinning a good story.

ANSWERS

Mostly A's
CREATIVE COSTUMER

You always want to make other people look and feel their best, even if it means more work for you. You are a unique individual always interested in trying new things. Plus, you have terrific fashion sense, so being a costumer is perfect for you.

Mostly B's
SPECTACULAR STUNTWOMAN

You have enough energy for five people and would never back down from a challenge. You prefer the thrill of trying something new to being the focus of people's attention. Courageous and creative, you would make a stunning stuntwoman.

Mostly C's
DYNAMITE DIRECTOR

You like to be the boss of every situation, and you have great leadership skills. With your knack for explaining things clearly, you'd be terrific at directing a film and getting the actors to make your vision come to life.

Mostly D's
SUPERB STAR

Being the center of attention suits you just fine. In fact, you're at your best when you're around a big group of people—you simply sparkle. People immediately take notice of you. With that kind of charisma, you'd be a very successful leading lady.

Meet Your Match

What qualities do you look for in the people you surround yourself with?

1 **If you could think of one word to describe your best friend, it would be:**

a. caring.

b. fun.

c. brilliant.

2 **You hate it when your friends:**

a. talk about other people behind their backs.

b. want to sit inside watching TV all day.

c. act silly.

3 **A really cute boy in your class got your attention by:**

a. offering you his seat on the bus one day.

b. inviting you to a party at his house.

c. giving a really cool oral presentation for a geography assignment.

4 **You finally score a date with your crush. But you totally lose interest when he:**

a. is rude to the waiter.

b. takes you to a stuffy restaurant.

c. can't hold a conversation with you.

7 You think _____ makes a guy really attractive.

  a. a kind heart

  b. fearlessness

  c. intelligence

8 You are having a conversation with someone for the very first time. You realize you are destined to be friends when he or she:

  a. is a good listener and respectful of your thoughts and stories.

  b. has the same interests as you.

  c. says something fascinating that makes you think.

5 Your parents let you bring a friend with you on your family vacation last year. Your favorite memory of the trip was:

  a. lying on the beach talking and reading magazines.

  b. going cliff jumping.

  c. visiting museums and shopping.

9 You've had a good day if you've:

  a. made a new friend.

  b. laughed so hard your cheeks started to ache.

  c. learned something new and exciting.

6 You and your friends can't stop talking about:

  a. how to get the new guy in history class to notice you.

  b. your weekend plans.

  c. the movie you just saw. It was amazing!

ANSWERS

Mostly A's
Loyal and True
You've got a huge heart and are always there for your friends. You would never leak a secret or make fun of a friend's feelings. That kind of loyalty in others is what draws you to them. You have no time for romance with a guy who trash-talks his buds.

Mostly B's
Gotta Have a Good Time
Fun is your middle name, and you get along best with people who love to laugh, play, and make the best of every situation. Your greatest fear is boredom. In friendship and flirting, you are looking for anyone who can make you smile.

Mostly C's
Incredible Intellect
You're one smart cookie and relate best to people who are as curious as you are. You love to discover new things and thrive on deep conversations with your friends. Any guy who makes you think about the world differently is worth your consideration.

41

Are You a GLOBE TREKKER?

Do you want to travel the world? Or is your own backyard the best place to be?

1 Your grandparents want to plan a monthlong vacation somewhere. You:

a. can't believe they'd even consider going away for so long. Won't they miss you?

b. offer to help them plan their trip. There are so many cool places that they should consider.

c. beg them to take you with them. You need a break from your normal, everyday life.

2 Your science teacher just returned from an African safari. You:

a. stay after class to ask him questions about the trip. How close did he get to the lions?

b. have no idea why anyone would want to go to Africa. Isn't it like 9,000 degrees there?

c. casually glance at his photos from the trip with your other classmates. You've never seen a kudu before!

3 Every Christmas, you and your family take a ten-hour car trip to your aunt's house for the holiday. You:

a. buy a stack of magazines and create a car trip playlist on your iPod. That'll help pass the time.

b. go online and search for places to stop along the way. A cool new gaming museum just opened that you want to check out.

c. ask your mom why your relatives can't ever come to your house. Fair's fair, right?

4 You have to do a geography report on a country that interests you. You choose:

a. Italy. You've been dreaming about going there since you were born and know everything about the place.

b. America. There's no place like home.

c. Cambodia. Don't they have cool temples there or something?

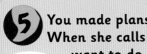

5 You made plans to hang out with a friend. When she calls to find out what you want to do, you:

   a. suggest that she come over to your house. Your mom picked up fresh strawberries and cream, and you've got a ton of new DVDs.

   b. leave it up to her. You're down with anything.

   c. ask her if she wants to try a new Turkish restaurant that opened in the next town over. You heard the food is fantastic!

6 You just recently starting writing to a pen pal. Where is she from?

   a. England
   b. India
   c. About an hour away

7 Your idea of the perfect vacation would be:

   a. visiting a place you've never been before.
   b. sailing around the world.
   c. hanging out at the beach your parents took you to every summer when you were a child. There are so many memories there.

8 Your uncle traveled to China for work. As a souvenir, you asked him to bring back:

   a. a tapestry for your wall.
   b. some chopsticks. You love Chinese food.
   c. a guidebook and tapes on speaking Chinese. If you pick up the language, maybe you could travel there, too.

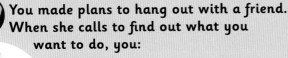

ANSWERS

1 a=1 b=2 c=3
2 a=3 b=1 c=2
3 a=2 b=3 c=1
4 a=3 b=1 c=2
5 a=1 b=2 c=3
6 a=2 b=3 c=1
7 a=2 b=3 c=1
8 a=2 b=1 c=3

20–24 points
UNSTOPPABLE EXPLORER

You're addicted to travel magazines and can't wait to visit the places you read about. You aren't afraid to try new cuisines. There's a whole wide world out there, and you plan to see every inch of it.

14–19 points
TESTING OUT TRAVEL

You are looking forward to visiting new places, but you'll be content checking out the rest of this country and maybe some European nations. You don't need to be halfway around the world to have an adventure.

8–13 points
HOMETOWN GIRL

You love where you live and are perfectly happy experiencing the beauty of your natural surroundings. Besides, with great books and Internet access, you never have to actually go to a place to learn about it.

Do You Stick Up for Yourself?

Do you fight for your rights or let others walk all over you? See where you stand.

1 You've got a super-bossy friend who has a habit of speaking for you. The next time she does this, you:

a. tell her that you have a voice too, and you'd like to use it.

b. pull her aside afterward and tell her that it really bothers you when she makes decisions for you.

c. say nothing. She means well.

2 A boy in your class keeps taunting you about how wimpy girls are compared to guys. You:

a. tell him brains beat brawn any day.

b. challenge him to an arm-wrestling match. You'll show him!

c. ignore him. Are boys always this obnoxious and annoying?

3 A friend borrowed lunch money from you three days in a row. That was two weeks ago. She still hasn't paid you back. You:

a. let it go. It's not that much money anyway.

b. ask to borrow money for a movie ticket and "forget" to pay her back. Now you're even.

c. simply ask her when she's going to pay you back. It was a loan, not a gift.

4 Your brother eats constantly and never leaves you any of the good snacks your mom buys. Next time you catch him swiping the last piece of chocolate cake, you:

a. grab the plate from him and throw it in the trash. Now, no one gets to have cake.

b. tell him you'd really appreciate it if he'd think before stuffing his face. You like to eat, too.

c. shoot him a dirty look and grab an apple instead. It's better for you anyway.

5 You find out one of your teammates has been talking about you behind your back. The next time you see her, you:

a. pull her aside and ask if you've done something to offend her.

b. loudly shout, "What, you can't talk about me to my face?"

c. avoid her. Maybe she's just having a bad day.

6 Your sister accidentally broke a neighbor's window. She asks you to take the blame so she won't miss an upcoming party. You:

a. tell her no way. She is responsible for her own screw-ups.

b. agree to be there when she tells your neighbor. She won't be in so much trouble if you both explain it was an accident.

c. do it. She's been looking forward to the weekend so much—you don't want her to miss out.

7 Your best friend has a habit of flirting with the guys you like. Next time you catch her with your crush, you:

a. assume they're talking about something harmless.

b. walk over and interrupt them. You are not going to let her have all the fun!

c. call her later and calmly discuss your feelings with her.

8 You're the captain of the cheerleading squad, but some of the members seem to think they're in charge. You:

a. let them think they have some power. You're not in the mood for a fight.

b. tell them that you're happy to have their input, but there's a reason you were elected captain.

c. suggest that if they have a problem taking orders, they shouldn't be on the squad.

9 You _____ confrontation.

a. hate

b. love

c. can handle

10 You wouldn't let your sister borrow your favorite jeans. Now she won't speak to you. You:

a. explain to her how heartbroken you'd be if anything happened to them.

b. accuse her of being a total baby.

c. cave and let her borrow the jeans. What's the worst that could happen?

ANSWERS

1	a=3	b=2	c=1
2	a=2	b=3	c=1
3	a=1	b=2	c=3
4	a=3	b=2	c=1
5	a=2	b=3	c=1
6	a=3	b=2	c=1
7	a=1	b=3	c=2
8	a=1	b=2	c=3
9	a=1	b=3	c=2
10	a=2	b=3	c=1

24–30 points
Looking Out For #1

You don't let anyone make you feel bad about yourself. But sometimes you're a little too defensive when sticking up for your rights, which can only make things worse. Try talking to people instead of yelling. They'll get the message.

17–23 points
Ain't No Doormat

You're great at letting people know when they've crossed a line with you. When you speak up, they listen, because you do it in a way that isn't offensive. And like the great friend that you are, you've got your pals' backs, too.

10–16 points
Suffering Silently

You're so afraid of getting into an argument, you'd rather let people disrespect you than tell them how you feel. But by letting people put you down, you're showing them that it's OK for them to treat you badly. It's not.

45

What Does YOUR 'DO Say About You?

Long, short, curly, or straight, your hair speaks volumes about your personality. What is yours saying?

1 Your favorite hair accessory is:

a. a sassy fake flower like the ones you see in the magazines.

b. a head scarf that you can wear loose or tight depending on your mood.

c. a scrunchie or elastic. You can wear it on your wrist when you don't need to put your hair up.

d. a barrette that blends in with your hair color.

2 When you try out new hair styles, there are:

a. plenty to experiment with. You love to try out the styles you see on the red carpet.

b. lots to try, but you don't like anything pulled too tight. Loose braids are way more your style.

c. a bunch that you can do, but you like to keep it simple. You're not that into using lots of accessories.

d. a lot that work with your hair, but they take so much effort, you probably wouldn't try them on a school day.

3 You cut your hair:

a. whenever there's a new trend.

b. hardly ever.

c. once a year.

d. every two to three months.

4 And when you do go to the hairdresser, it's usually:

a. a drastic change.

b. several inches. Your mom always bugs you when your locks start looking messy.

c. hardly noticeable. Your hair always looks good.

d. a tiny trim, just to get rid of your split ends.

5 Your friend bought semi-permanent purple hair dye for both of you. When she offers you some, you:

a. color a couple of strands underneath your hair.

b. color your entire head. This is going to look so cool.

c. try some highlights on top. You'll have a cool glow in the right light!

d. say no thanks. If God wanted you to have purple hair, you would have been born with it.

ANSWERS

Mostly A's	Mostly B's	Mostly C's	Mostly D's
FOLLOWS FASHION	**FREE SPIRIT**	**NATURAL BEAUTY**	**PRETTY PRACTICAL**
If Mohawks were back in style, you'd run right out and get one. You're a slave to style, and your hair reflects that. You always look very fresh and current.	Long and flowing or short and sassy, your locks are a symbol of your sunny disposition and laid-back attitude. You don't let anything stress you out, and you hate complications.	You've got gorgeous hair, but it mainly just gets in your way. You're an active person and don't spend a lot of time agonizing over your appearance. Your self-confidence shines.	You don't like change (which is probably why you've had the same hairstyle since first grade). You're a serious person, and you don't really get caught up with every new trend.

For a **MILLION** Dollars...

How far would you go?

Circle each thing that you'd do if the prize were $1,000,000.

- Shave your head

- Roll around in dog poop

- Go bungee jumping

- Let a tarantula crawl on you for five minutes

- Remain silent for an entire month

- Go on a hunger strike for a week

 • Eat a live cockroach

- Blend a raw egg, onions, ketchup, orange juice, and milk together and then drink it

- Never speak to your best friend ever again

- Walk naked down the hallway at school

- Cut off your sister's hair while she slept

- Spend a night in a cemetery by yourself

- Drink a whole bottle of olive oil

- Tell your crush that you're madly in love with him

- Agree not to drive a car until you are thirty

- Get a tattoo on your forehead

- Dress like a clown—nose and all—for a year

- Spend a month on a deserted tropical island

> Now give yourself one point for every scenario you circled.

YOUR SCORE:

14–18 points
FEARLESS FORTUNE HUNTER

Whether you are crazy for cash or always up for a dare, you would trounce the competition in any contest of courage. The question is: What would you buy first?

7–13 points
MAYBE FOR MORE

A million dollars is really appealing, but there are some things that you just can't bring yourself to go through with. But for $5 million, maybe…

0–6 points
SO NOT WORTH IT

You'd love to be rich, but you won't go to just any lengths to do so. Who would eat live bugs or lay down in dog poop? Can you say "gross"?

47

Are You A COUCH POTATO?
Is "lazy" your middle name? Or are you a busy, busy bee?

START

Your alarm goes off at 7:30 a.m. to wake you up for school. You:

bound out of bed eager to start your day.

keep hitting snooze until your mom has to drag you out of bed.

roll over and go back to sleep for fifteen precious minutes.

You just got home from school. What do you do?

Grab a snack and start your homework

Flip on your favorite soap opera

hit pause and head to the refrigerator.

Your friend asks you to go for a bike ride with her. You:

will have to wait. You are really getting into the plot.

Your idea of exercising is:

walking around the mall.

going to the gym for an hour or two.

You're watching a movie and want some milk. You:

yell for your mom to bring you a glass.

If you are sitting in your room, you are usually:

You're at the town pool. What do you spend the day doing?

Doing laps

Swimming and sunning

Lying on your lounge chair

reading a good book.

daydreaming.

tell her you heard about a new trail that's supposed to be really challenging.

agree, but only if it's a short one, and you can get cheesesteaks afterwards.

You have to run a mile in gym in order to pass the class. You:

make it most of the way through, but then have to slow down to a walk.

politely decline. You always feel great after a workout.

try to break a school record while you're at it.

You are contemplating working out, but your friend calls and asks if you want to come over and watch a movie. You:

decide to go to your friend's house. You can go for a jog tomorrow.

gladly accept. Phew! This way you don't have to go to the gym.

It's a lovely day outside, and your family wants to go on a picnic. You:

volunteer to make the sandwiches.

fake sick and spend the day playing video games.

BUNDLE OF ENERGY

Do you ever sleep? You love to be on the go, and if you can get some exercise in the process, all the better. Sitting still makes you restless, so you try to pack your days with stuff to do.

EFFORT TO BE ACTIVE

You're pretty good about getting some exercise, although sometimes you just need a day to veg out in a comfy chair with a good book. There's nothing wrong with that. Everyone needs a rest sometimes.

LAZY WITH A CAPITAL "L"

Does your couch have a permanent dent in it from where your butt always is? You're wasting your life away in front of the TV. Try getting outside sometime. The fresh air will be good for you.

How AMBITIOUS Are You?

Are you shooting for the treetops or the stars?

1 When you grow up, you want to be:

   a. well respected in your chosen field.

   b. the first female president.

   c. financially secure.

2 Tryouts for soccer are next week. You're hoping to:

   a. make the team.

   b. be chosen for the goalie spot.

   c. be elected captain.

3 You've got a really hard math test coming up. How long have you been studying for it?

   a. You haven't started yet. You know enough to get at least a B.

   b. A few days. You try to review a little bit each night.

   c. Almost two weeks. You're going to ace this exam if it kills you!

4 In order to get a passing grade in your art class, you have to make at least one pottery project. How many do you hand in?

   a. Two

   b. Six

   c. One

5 Your school's talent show is coming up, and you find out that first prize is $100. You:

   a. start practicing a powerful ballad. You think you have a chance to win.

   b. ask your best friend if she'll do a karaoke duet with you. It could be a lot of fun.

   c. agree to sing backup for a friend. If you win, you can split the pot.

6 **You make sure to exercise:**

a. a couple of times a week.

b. every day.

c. hardly ever.

7 **You get a summer job to have money for:**

a. a cute new school-year wardrobe.

b. snacks when you and your friends go out.

c. your future car.

8 **Someday you plan to live:**

a. anywhere your parents don't.

b. in a big city.

c. . . .well, it depends on the time of year. You plan on having more than one home.

9 **You'll get married:**

a. by age 26. You want to have your first child by age 28.

b. when you find the right person.

c. maybe never. You haven't really thought about it.

10 **Class rankings are coming out soon. You hope to be:**

a. passing.

b. number one.

c. in the top ten percent.

#1

ANSWERS

1 a=2	b=3	c=1
2 a=1	b=2	c=3
3 a=1	b=2	c=3
4 a=2	b=3	c=1
5 a=3	b=2	c=1
6 a=2	b=3	c=1
7 a=2	b=1	c=3
8 a=1	b=2	c=3
9 a=3	b=2	c=1
10 a=1	b=3	c=2

24–30 points
SHOOTING STAR

You give 110 percent to everything you do and have really high standards for yourself. If you can't be the best at something, it's not worth doing. As a result, you put a lot of pressure on yourself. Remember to enjoy your days and not to concentrate all of your effort on your future—you don't want to get stressed out.

17–23 points
HIGH HOPES

You want to be successful, but you're not the type of person who's going to chain herself to a desk to do so, which means you will have a nice quality of life. You don't have to be the head of the company to do a good job. You always give things your best try because you know that's all you can do.

10–16 points
JUST ENOUGH TO GET BY

You don't push yourself at all. While you won't let yourself fail, you do the bare minimum to succeed. You're not a big goal setter and prefer to just let things happen. The great thing about setting realistic goals is how great you feel when you achieve them. You should try it some time!

What's Your **HABITAT**?

In what kind of environment are you destined to do well?

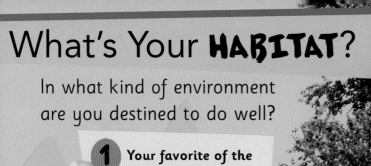

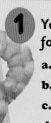

1 **Your favorite of the following foods is:**
- **a.** shrimp.
- **b.** hamburgers.
- **c.** oranges.
- **d.** ice cream.
- **e.** granola bars.

2 **Your mom lets you help choose the locale for the next family vacation. You start researching:**
- **a.** island-hopping in the Caribbean.
- **b.** a road trip across the United States.
- **c.** exploring the jungles and beaches of Costa Rica.
- **d.** skiing and snowboarding in the Alps.
- **e.** camping in the Rockies.

3 **When the weather's right, one of your favorite things to do is:**
- **a.** swim in the ocean.
- **b.** play in the park.
- **c.** explore the wooded park nearby.
- **d.** make snow angels.
- **e.** go rock climbing.

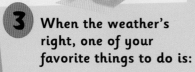

4 **You think it'd be fun to spend a month living in a:**
- **a.** submarine.
- **b.** barn.
- **c.** tree house.
- **d.** igloo.
- **e.** mountain cabin.

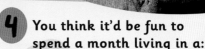

5 **You would jump at the chance to join a _____ club.**
- **a.** diving
- **b.** track
- **c.** gymnastics
- **d.** figure skating
- **e.** kayaking

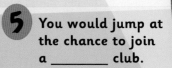

6 **It's 90 degrees out. What are you doing?**
- **a.** Running through the hose in your front yard
- **b.** Taking a nap on a lawn chair
- **c.** Reading in the shade of your favorite tree
- **d.** Sitting inside in the air conditioning
- **e.** Hiking

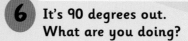

7 If you auditioned for a reality show, which would you choose?

a. *Surfin' Safari*, where groups live on a boat and sail to their coastal challenges, which may include swimming contests, water-ski jumps, underwater scavenger hunts, and all-you-can-eat seafood feasts

b. *Ranch Rangers*, where kids must prove they can live off the land, rising with the sun, racing horses across the plains, lassoing calves, farming for food, and enjoying the wide open sky

c. *Amazin' Amazon*, where two teams race through the jungle to reach a treasure, hiking through dense green forests, climbing trees, spotting exotic wildlife, and eating the freshest fruits on earth

d. *Arctic Adventures*, where rival teams compete in icy tasks during two months in the snowy wilderness, complete with ice fishing, snowshoe races, and warming up by the fire

e. *Summit Seekers*, where teens from all over the world try to outdo one another on a quest to reach a mountaintop, complete with hiking, animal-tracking, cliff-jumping, and sharing campfire stories

8 Your favorite color is:

a. blue.

b. orange.

c. green.

d. white.

e. yellow.

ANSWERS

Mostly A's
WATER BABY
Whether you're swimming, snorkeling, or lounging on the beach, you're all about the aquatic life. You're in the dumps if you're not near water. If you weren't a person, you'd love living in the sea as a dolphin or a sea otter. With your water mania, you should think about being a marine biologist, dolphin trainer, sailing instructor, or even seaside B&B owner.

Mostly B's
HORSING AROUND
You love open spaces and being under a bright blue sky. You're also sleek and poised, like a beautiful stallion. You enjoy freedom and do not need lots of fancy things to amuse you. You are just as happy hanging with your friends as you are walking the dog or kicking around a ball with your siblings. Whatever you do, you're sure to be surrounded by land.

Mostly C's
MONKEY BUSINESS
You'd jump at the chance to live in a rain forest. You are flexible and daring, like the chimps that swing around in the tropical canopies. Being surrounded by greenery and bright, exotic flowers is exciting for you. Trees are beautiful to you, so you're always at home taking a stroll in the forest and listening to the buzzing and cawing of the animals.

Mostly D's
BEARING UP
You are the only one you know that thrives when the temperature drops below 40 degrees. And not just for the snow days. You love the cold wind whipping through your hair. Whether you are on a sled, a snowboard, or a pair of skis or snowshoes, you're happiest in chilly surroundings. You should live up north, where you can enjoy rosy cheeks and hot chocolate all year long!

Mostly E's
MOUNTAIN LION
Seeing the sights from a mountain summit has always been a draw for you. You would rather rock-climb or hang-glide—anything that lets you hike or soar far above the rest of the world energizes you. Your habitat is mountain terrain, and if you can't live near a mountain range, you might want to work at a ski resort or consider becoming a trail guide one day.

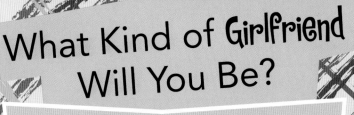

What Kind of Girlfriend Will You Be?

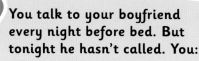

Needy, nurturing, or just plain nice? What's your couple style?

1 You talk to your boyfriend every night before bed. But tonight he hasn't called. You:

a. text him ten times and then contemplate asking for a ride to his house to make sure he's still alive.

b. figure he's probably had a rough day and is too tired to talk.

c. leave him a voicemail wishing him sweet dreams.

2 His soccer team just won the state championship. After the game, he says you can join him to celebrate with his friends. You:

a. happily go along with him. You don't want to miss out on the fun!

b. beg him not to go. You were really looking forward to spending some alone time with him.

c. tell him to go on without you. He should share this triumph with his team. You'll see him tomorrow.

3 His grades are slipping in English class, and he really needs to read and study more. You:

a. offer to write his next paper for him.

b. complain that he's neglecting you when he can't hang out.

c. respect the fact that his grades matter to him and give him space to get his work done.

4 It's your birthday and to celebrate, he gives you a beautiful locket. You:

a. love it. You feel like the luckiest girl in the world.

b. feel guilty that he spent so much money on you.

c. thank him but remind him that your mom's planning a family dinner tonight, and he better be there—with flowers.

5 When he has free time, you expect him to:

a. spend it doing something he likes.

b. spend it with you.

c. spend some of it hanging out with you.

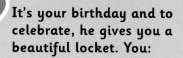

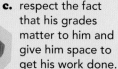

6 ♥ He gets a new puppy, but his mom says it's his responsibility to take care of it. You:

a. offer to help him take the cute pooch on walks whenever he wants company.

b. can't wait to play with it.

c. feel like he pays more attention to the dog than he does to you.

7 ♥ You see him talking to another girl in class. You:

a. go over and join the conversation. She seems nice.

b. demand to know what he was talking to her about.

c. wait for him to finish. They're probably just talking about homework, and you don't want him to think you don't trust him.

8 ♥ He made plans with you, but then his friend calls with tickets to his favorite team's game. When he breaks plans with you, you:

a. refuse to speak to him for a week. That'll show him.

b. are upset, but don't make a big fuss about it.

c. tell him he'd better go! It is his favorite team—and he shouldn't pass up great seats.

ANSWERS

1 a=1 b=3 c=2
2 a=2 b=1 c=3
3 a=2 b=1 c=3
4 a=3 b=2 c=1
5 a=2 b=1 c=3
6 a=2 b=3 c=1
7 a=3 b=1 c=2
8 a=1 b=2 c=3

20–24 points
One Great Gal
Any guy would love to go out with you because you're warm, caring, and laid-back, and you won't make him feel guilty for not spending every moment with you. You understand that for a relationship to work, you have to have your own lives, as well as have fun when you are together.

14–19 points
Helpful Honey
If you love someone, of course you want to support and take care of him. But it sounds like sometimes you might go a little too far by wanting to do everything for him. When you start dating someone, make sure your helpful instinct doesn't take away from the fun you should be having.

8–13 points
Needy Nag
Be careful! Just because a guy does not want to see you 24/7, it doesn't mean he's not into you. Everyone needs time with friends and time alone. And if you don't give it to him, he may stop hanging out with you permanently. So, when you snag a BF, make sure to give him some space, too.

If You Joined The Circus...

What role would you play under the big top?

1 You're at a party with kids from school. What are you doing?

a. Playing DJ

b. Trying to get a game of truth or dare going

c. Juggling your friends' hats

d. Singing karaoke

e. Checking out the cutie in the corner

2 You're making a movie in film class. What position do you choose?

a. Director

b. Location scout

c. Comic relief

d. Leading lady

e. Script writer

3 If you could pick the ideal summer job, which of these would you choose?

a. Starting a dog-walking service

b. Working with wild animals at the zoo

c. Performing at children's birthday parties

d. Teaching ballet

e. Being a tour guide at a museum

4 It really annoys you when other people:

a. can't make decisions.

b. aren't willing to try new things.

c. have no sense of humor.

d. steal the spotlight.

e. talk too much.

5 Your best friend just broke up with her boyfriend. To cheer her up, you:

a. introduce her to your super-cute cousin.

b. drag her to a spinning class. She'll be able to get her frustrations out on the bike.

c. do your impression of your science teacher. That always cracks her up.

d. take her to the spa for a day.

e. let her talk and cry until she feels better.

6 There's a really shy girl in your class who sits alone at lunch every day. The next time you see her, you:

a. invite her to come sit with you and your friends.

b. go over to her table and ask if you can join her.

c. make a joke about how loud and obnoxious you must seem to her.

d. figure there must be a reason she doesn't have any friends.

e. wonder if she prefers being alone.

7 In your circle of friends, you're known as:

a. the planner.

b. the girl who'll try anything.

c. the funny one.

d. the drama queen.

e. the listener.

8 Someday you want to:

a. own your own business.

b. climb Mount Everest.

c. have an MTV hidden-camera show.

d. be the next American Idol.

e. publish a novel.

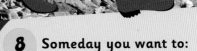

ANSWERS

Mostly A's
Ringmaster Royale
Your friends look to you as their leader, and you kind of like being in charge. You know how to make things happen and can tell people what to do without being too bossy.

Mostly B's
Terrific Trapeze Artist
Soaring through the air with nothing between you and the ground but a net is the perfect job for you. You love adventure. The adrenaline rush you get is well worth the risk.

Mostly C's
Comical Clown
If you can make someone smile or laugh, you've had a wonderful day. You're naturally fun and entertaining and have no problem making a fool of yourself in front of others.

Mostly Ds
Tantalizing Tightrope Walker
You are completely comfortable when all eyes are on you. Stylish and graceful, you are a poised performer. With your talent and timing, you would shine walking the rope.

Mostly E's
Clever Fortune-Teller
You prefer to sit back and observe the world rather than be the center of it. Because of this, you are a great judge of character. Quick-witted and loyal, you give the best advice.

57

How Well Do You **KNOW** Your Friends?

Take this either/or quiz to see how well you know your friends. Make copies of this quiz and share with your friends. For each pair on the list, circle the item or activity you would prefer. Then circle the one your friend would pick. Compare your answers. Give yourself a point if your guess matches her circle. Your friend also gets a point for correctly guessing your picks.

WHICH ONE DOES MY FRIEND LIKE?

My friend's name is _____

Chocolate or vanilla?

Summer or winter?

Read the book or watch the movie?

Outgoing or shy?

Tiny sports car or huge SUV?

City pad or beach bungalow?

Scrabble® or Monopoly®?

French fries or potato chips?

French fries or chocolate mousse?

Cell phone or iPod?

Drawing or knitting?

Scrapbooking or ski-jumping?

Hiking or jogging?

WHICH ONE DO I LIKE?

My name is _____

Chocolate or vanilla?

Summer or winter?

Read the book or watch the movie?

Outgoing or shy?

Tiny sports car or huge SUV?

City pad or beach bungalow?

Scrabble® or Monopoly®?

French fries or potato chips?

French fries or chocolate mousse?

Cell phone or iPod?

Drawing or knitting?

Scrapbooking or ski-jumping?

Hiking or jogging?

Snorkeling or scuba diving?

Scuba diving or skydiving?

Rock or rap?

Country or pop?

Lipstick or lip balm?

Hair up or hair down?

Mexican food or Chinese food?

Action film or romantic comedy?

History or sci-fi?

Spend it or save it?

Morning person or late sleeper?

Dogs or cats?

Parakeet or goldfish?

Marching band or choir?

Football or baseball?

Ballet or jazz dance?

Wear black or wear pink?

Snorkeling or scuba diving?

Scuba diving or skydiving?

Rock or rap?

Country or pop?

Lipstick or lip balm?

Hair up or hair down?

Mexican food or Chinese food?

Action film or romantic comedy?

History or sci-fi?

Spend it or save it?

Morning person or late sleeper?

Dogs or cats?

Parakeet or goldfish?

Marching band or choir?

Football or baseball?

Ballet or jazz dance?

Wear black or wear pink?

21–30 points

SOUL SISTERS

Wow, you know your friend really well. Can you predict what movie you two are going to see next? You are very observant and spend a lot of time listening to what she has to say. It looks like you two will be friends for a long time to come.

11–20 points

NOT SO PSYCHIC SIDEKICK

One of the great parts about friendship is that as you continue to spend time together, you will keep on learning cool things about each other. You already know some stuff about your friend but can always pick up more about her likes and dislikes.

0–10 points

WHAT'S YOUR NAME AGAIN?

Did you two just meet? Maybe you should take a few minutes to remind each other about your vitals—what's your favorite color, food, band, and movie? Once you start sharing, you'll key into each other's personality and what makes you tick.

What's Your Sense of Style?

Pretend you are in a clothing store and can only pick ten of the following items. Circle the ones you would choose, and see which column has the most circles.

Column A

A rhinestone-decorated tank top

A bunch of shimmery bangles

Strappy leopard-print heels

A funky skirt with a matching chain belt

Fitted jeans

A T-shirt with your favorite band's logo on it

A fuzzy, touchable scarf

Platform sneakers

A zip-up hoodie with a bold pattern

A wacky tiered skirt

Column B

Super-high black heels

Black sunglasses

Tan capri pants

A black skirt

A cashmere sweater

Hand-beaded shirt

Gray pants

Boot-cut jeans

Bronze flip-flops

A flirty skirt

Column C

Blue hoodie

Green track pants

Silver high-tops

Flared jeans

A colorful turtleneck sweater

Black leather boots

Ski jacket

Tank tops in a rainbow of colors

Purple sports bra

Red running shoes

Column D

Lace blouse

Ruffled pink skirt

A flowery halter top

Decorated jeans with matching fabric belt

Ballet flats

A flirty sundress

Wrap skirt

Monogrammed sweater

A heart-shaped necklace

Faux diamond earrings

Answers

Column B
Classic Look

You prefer simple lines and sophisticated colors when you shop for clothes. And you don't mind buying well-made, expensive pieces because you know you'll wear them forever.

Column A
Style Statement

You change your look a lot, because it is exciting for you to experiment with different fashion personalities. You don't shy from wild patterns or cutting-edge looks. If it is fresh and funky, it's for you.

Column C
Athletic Accents

You're always on the go, so it's important that you feel comfortable in your clothes. But that doesn't mean you don't want to look cool, too. Hip takes on jeans and sweatpants are in your zone.

Column D
Girl Power

You embrace your femininity, and your look reflects that. You love to wear skirts and dresses, and your closet contains all the colors of cotton candy. Soft, touchable fabrics are also a draw for you.

Are You a SURVIVOR?

Would you make it if you were stranded on a deserted island or all alone in a foreign land?

START

Imagine you are shipwrecked but manage to swim to shore. What's the first thing you do?

Gather sticks to build a fire

Sunbathe. You might as well get a tan while you are here.

Find a fruit tree and have a snack. You're starving!

The scariest part about spending a night in a tent in the woods is:

the thought that a bear might be interested in the food you packed.

...um, everything. There are bugs and animals, and what if there is a werewolf or a psycho on the loose?

hoping you packed enough bug spray. Mosquito bites are so itchy!

At summer camp, your cabin has a list of tasks to complete in order to win the camp championship. Which one of these two tasks would you pick?

Make trail mix for the two-mile hike your teammates will be taking

Swim the length of the entire lake and back

What's the toughest meal you think you could handle?

On a class trip to Italy, you get separated from your group. Your Italian is awful, and you lost your emergency phone number list, so you:

sit in a café with a map and a cup of strong coffee. If you concentrate, you are sure you can figure this out.

wander back and forth on your route. Eventually, someone will realize you're missing and come look for you, right?

You're sunbathing on a raft when you realize that you have drifted really far from the beach. What do you do?

Eating the squished, three-day-old granola bar that was in the bottom of your bag

Catching and cooking a fish

For school, you have to participate in a community service project. You have been assigned to help fix up a house. You:

This is the last straw! You will sit down and wait for them to come back or someone can walk you back to the campsite.

look forward to it. You'll get a good workout and maybe meet some new people.

beg your teacher for something that will require less sweating. Maybe you could fold brochures for a good cause?

NOT-SO-TOUGH COOKIE

You panic at the mere thought of a crisis. Just getting a hangnail could make you hysterical. Even though the great outdoors aren't your thing, maybe you should check out a survival guide—you know, just in case.

You are on a hiking trip when you realize that you will need to do some rock climbing to get to the next part of the trail. How do you react?

Sweet! This is so exciting. You've never climbed this high up before.

You are a little frightened, but know how great it will feel when you reach the top.

Start the long swim back to shore

Panic and hope that the lifeguard will hear your shouting. You'd rather be rescued than brave the water.

You have to switch planes on your way to visit relatives. When your connecting flight is canceled, you:

You are on a reality show, and in order to win the first challenge, your team needs to build a shelter. What do you do?

Try to look busy so no one will ask you to carry anything heavy

Collect logs that can be used as supports and start digging holes for them in the ground. You'll make the sturdiest "house" on the show.

go to the airline counter and try to get on the next flight.

Find some leafy branches for the thatched roof. It's helpful, but not as hard as helping to build the frame.

call your parents, explain the situation, and ask them to take care of it.

ROUGH AND READY

You'd be the best person to have in a sticky situation because you always know what to do in a crisis. You are not afraid to get your hands dirty or to work hard to get things done. You are a true survivor!

SOMEWHAT STRONG

You are always willing to help in a pinch, but scaling mountains and braving the wilderness aren't your idea of fun. You try to keep a cool head in difficult scenarios, but that's not always easy when you're scared.

What's Your PERFECT PROFESSION?

Not sure what you want to be when you grow up? Take this quiz to see what career suits you.

1 Looking around your bedroom, a person would probably guess that you:

a. are extremely neat and clean.

b. are really into high-tech gadgets.

c. have amazing taste.

d. love kids.

2 One of your chores is to help your mom with dinner every night. You're really good at:

a. dicing the vegetables for stir-fry. Yummy!

b. deciding what dishes she should make.

c. setting the table.

d. baking cupcakes for dessert.

3 In school, you excel at:

a. biology.

b. math.

c. home economics.

d. English.

4 You just got home from school. What do you do first?

a. Start your homework. Your teachers really piled it on tonight.

b. Answer some emails and check in with friends over IM

c. Work on the curtains you've been sewing for your room. They're going to look so cool.

d. Pick up the book you've been reading. You've been wondering about the characters all day and can't wait to find out what happens.

5 You're at your school's book fair and only have enough money for one item. What do you choose?

a. A book on the human body

b. A biography of a successful woman

c. A catalog of DIY projects

d. A collection of children's fairy tales

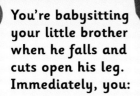

6 You're babysitting your little brother when he falls and cuts open his leg. Immediately, you:

a. apply pressure to the wound to stop the bleeding.

b. call your mom.

c. take a deep breath. You hate the sight of blood.

d. sing him a song to take his mind off the pain.

7 Out of your group of friends, you're definitely the most:

a. intelligent.

b. bossy.

c. stylish.

d. easygoing.

8 It's supposed to rain all weekend. You decide to use your time stuck indoors to:

a. work on your project for the science fair.

b. start thinking about your campaign for class president.

c. paint a mural on your wall.

d. read.

ANSWERS

Mostly A's
EMERGENCY SERVICE

You're very disciplined and hardworking, which is exactly what every aspiring doctor, EMT, or policewoman must be. With your ability to work under pressure and that huge brain of yours, you're going to save lives someday.

Mostly B's
CEO IN THE MAKING

Politics and business are two great options for you. You're smart and savvy and know how to get what you want. Plus, you're completely in tune with technology and know how to balance many things at once.

Mostly C's
DESIGN DIVA

Your creativity and great eye for detail will help you excel as an interior decorator, fashion designer, or artist. Your friends always want your opinion on their clothes, hair, or furniture—and someday you'll get paid for that!

Mostly D's
TEACHER OF THE YEAR

You have a ton of patience and love little kids, so teaching is a natural fit for you. Whether you are a camp counselor, storyteller, teacher, or child psychologist, you'll put your kid-friendly talents to work.

Do You Give in to PEER PRESSURE?

Would you do anything just to be popular?

1 You're invited to a really popular girl's birthday. People are buying her super-expensive gifts, but you don't have lots of money. You:

a. ask two friends if they want to go in on a designer gift together.

b. beg your parents to help out. You don't want to look like a loser.

c. look for something nice in your normal birthday budget range.

2 At the drugstore, you see your cousin slip a bunch of lip glosses and eye shadows into her backpack. You:

a. discreetly walk out of the store. What she did is wrong, but you wouldn't mind trying some of those shadows.

b. pray that you don't get caught for being with her.

c. tell her to put them back immediately. Is she crazy?

3 Everyone at school makes fun of this one overweight kid. When you walk past him, you:

a. don't say anything, but laugh when other people call him funny names.

b. say "What's up fatty?" like the others.

c. frown at the girls who call him names. Kids can be so mean.

4 Everyone is buying a brand of pricey sneakers that you find kind of ugly. You:

a. buy them in a different color than everyone else.

b. pony up the money. You would rather fit in than not.

c. refuse to spend money on something you hate.

5 You're at the park when a classmate pulls out a permanent marker and writes on the wall. When he hands you the pen, you:

a. tell him you're a horrible drawer and you'll pass.

b. make a big heart with your and your crush's initials.

c. ask him why he wants to graffiti such a beautiful park.

ANSWERS

Mostly A's
PASSIVE PERSON

While you don't always give in to your peers, you don't always speak up. The next time someone upsets you, summon the courage to tell him what you think.

Mostly B's
COMPLETE CAVER

You want people to like you so badly that you'll do anything to please them. Start thinking for yourself. Your friends might not always be there for you—and they may get you in real trouble someday.

Mostly C's
ALWAYS YOUR OWN WOMAN

You have terrific self-esteem, and you never let anyone make you feel pressured. You realize that they'll respect you more for sticking to your beliefs. You should encourage this confidence in others.

What SEASON Sings to You?

Winter, spring, summer, or fall? What does your favorite season say about your personality?

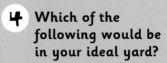

1 You love looking out your window and seeing:

   a. a blanket of fresh white snow on the ground.

   b. bright budding flowers.

   c. the aqua-colored water of your pool.

   d. brilliant orange, red, and yellow leaves.

2 Your favorite thing to drink is:

   a. hot chocolate.

   b. iced coffee.

   c. lemonade.

   d. spicy chai tea.

3 You feel most comfortable in:

   a. a cozy sweater.

   b. a pastel-colored skirt and sleeveless top.

   c. a tank top and shorts.

   d. jeans and a crisp blazer.

4 Which of the following would be in your ideal yard?

   a. A great hill for sledding

   b. A pretty gazebo with vines growing on one side

   c. A huge sprinkler in the yard

   d. A campfire to sit around in the evening

5 One of your favorite activities is:

   a. skiing.

   b. riding your bike.

   c. swimming.

   d. hiking.

6 Your family might describe you as:

   a. quiet.

   b. nurturing.

   c. lazy.

   d. private.

Mostly A's
WINTER WOMAN

You find winter the most peaceful season. Everything is quiet and beautiful, much like yourself. You are a patient person who loves to frolic in the snow and then burrow under a blanket, safe and warm.

Mostly B's
SPRING IN YOUR STEP

Spring is a time of new beginnings, when flowers and trees come to life. You find the spring showers and budding greenery extremely refreshing. You're an encouraging friend with a positive attitude.

Mostly C's
SUMMER LOVIN'

You're casual and fun and love the slow pace of summer. Everyone just looks healthier and happier. Plus, you love the outdoors and being active. And not having to go to school isn't bad either!

Mostly D's
FABULOUS FALL

When the air starts to turn crisp as summer comes to an end, you feel most alive. Not too hot and not too cold, the temperature is just right for someone with your keen sense of observation and sharp wit.

How Adventurous Are You?

Are you willing to try new things, or is safe and steady more your speed?

1 Your idea of "roughing it" is:

    a. sleeping in a cheap motel.

    b. sleeping in a tent.

    c. sleeping in the wilderness under the stars.

2 You're at a fancy restaurant, and your aunt orders frogs' legs. When the order arrives, you:

    a. gingerly take a bite. They probably taste like chicken.

    b. make sure they're as far away from you as possible. Eww!

    c. wait for your brother to try them first.

3 Your best friend's family is going sailing for a year on a small boat. They've asked you to come along. You:

    a. start researching remedies for seasickness. It is curable right?

    b. beg your parents to let you go. This is the chance of a lifetime.

    c. say thanks, but no thanks. You know nothing about sailing and don't care to.

4 Some of your friends have gotten really into Pilates. When they ask you to come to a class, you:

    a. would love to but tell them you don't know when you'll have time with all of your activities.

    b. aren't into it. Don't they stretch you on a rack or something crazy like that?

    c. tell them to name the time and place. It could be fun!

5 What is the fastest you would ever want to go?

    a. You'd try out one of those astronaut machines that swings you around at like a million miles an hour!

    b. Driving a race car would be fun.

    c. Galloping on a horse is fast enough for you.

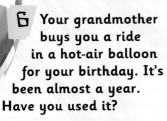

6 Your grandmother buys you a ride in a hot-air balloon for your birthday. It's been almost a year. Have you used it?

a. No way. You can't even control those things.

b. Of course. In fact, you used it within a week of getting her gift.

c. Not yet, but you plan on going soon.

7 When it comes to finding a summer job, you:

a. want to do something wild like work in an amusement park.

b. start looking in the classifieds, but know you can always work for your folks if you don't find anything.

c. go back to the place where you worked last year. At least you'll know what to expect there.

8 Your friend's birthday is on Halloween, and she's having her party at a haunted house at the end of a really dark, spooky street. Do you go?

a. Maybe, but only if a huge group of guys is going with you

b. Definitely. You've always been curious about what kind of show they put on down there.

c. Not on your life. It's too risky. You don't want to be remembered as the girl who ran screaming from a birthday party.

9 During a school getaway to a lake, each student gets to choose from a menu of cool outdoor activities. Which is the craziest you would go for?

a. Canoeing

b. Parasailing

c. Water-skiing

ANSWERS

1 a=1 b=2 c=3
2 a=3 b=1 c=2
3 a=2 b=3 c=1
4 a=2 b=1 c=3
5 a=3 b=2 c=1
6 a=1 b=3 c=2
7 a=3 b=2 c=1
8 a=2 b=3 c=1
9 a=1 b=3 c=2

21–27 points
Gutsy Gal

You live for excitement and are always willing to try new things, whether that means eating exotic foods or traveling to strange lands. You truly believe that life is a journey, and you want yours to be action-packed.

15–20 points
Adventurer-in-Training

You don't like to be bored and are curious about the world, so you're often willing to try new activities. But some things are a little too outlandish. You'd be just fine living your life without trying calves' brains or skydiving.

9–14 points
Lily-Livered Lass

You are perfectly happy the way you are and don't like going outside of your comfort zone. If something scares you or grosses you out, you gladly take that as a sign that you're not meant to do it.

Are You **Too Quiet?**

Are you a woman of few words or do you have the gift of gab?

1 You get in trouble for talking in class:

  a. pretty much everyday.

  b. once in a while.

  c. never.

2 Every night your best friend calls you before bed. How long do you talk?

  a. A minute or less. You saw her all day in school, so you don't have much to catch up on.

  b. Ten or fifteen minutes. You need to discuss the plotline of your favorite show.

  c. Until your parents yell at you to get off the phone and go to bed

3 Your dad comes to pick you up from school. As soon as you get in the car, you:

  a. tell him about the grade you got on your history test.

  b. turn up the radio. You just want to zone out.

  c. give him a detailed description of everything that happened to you since you saw him this morning.

4 You're in the waiting room at the dentist's office, and there's a cute boy sitting next to you. When he says hello, you:

  a. pretend to be really engrossed in the magazine you're reading.

  b. say hi and reply when he asks where you go to school.

  c. say hello and ask him what he's doing there. Then you tell him all about the cavity you're getting filled.

5 You have to do a group presentation about geography. You volunteer to:

  a. do the introduction.

  b. type up the report if it means you don't have to say anything.

  c. give the entire presentation.

6 You are at a pizza place hanging out with your friends after a game. When your parents come to pick you up, you:

  a. ask them to wait five more minutes so you can finish up your conversation.

  b. beg them to let a few of your friends come over so you guys can keep talking and laughing about the game.

  c. are always ready to go on time.

7 Every month you _____ your cell phone minutes.

a. barely dent

b. go over

c. almost use up

8 You just found out that your older sister, who lives a few hours away from you, got an amazing, high-paying new job. You:

a. tell her you want to hear all about it when she starts.

b. say congratulations the next time she visits.

c. start shrieking about how excited you are for her, grab the phone, and call with a million questions about her new life.

9 You love going to the library because:

a. that's where everyone hangs out.

b. your crush is always there.

c. it's very peaceful, and you love to read.

10 Your dad is hosting a surprise anniversary party for your mom. When he asks you to say a few words to the crowd, you:

a. simply tell your folks how much you love them both.

b. eagerly grab the microphone and regale their friends with stories of how wonderful your parents are (and how they love to embarrass you).

c. vigorously shake your head no and volunteer your brother instead.

ANSWERS

1 a=1 b=2 c=3

2 a=3 b=2 c=1

3 a=2 b=3 c=1

4 a=3 b=2 c=1

5 a=2 b=3 c=1

6 a=2 b=1 c=3

7 a=3 b=1 c=2

8 a=2 b=3 c=1

9 a=1 b=2 c=3

10 a=2 b=1 c=3

24–30 points
Quiet as a Mouse

You're so quiet people sometimes forget you're even in the room! While it's just as important to listen, you shouldn't be afraid to say what you think or feel. People are interested in your views, too.

17–23 points
Sensible Speaker

You're not a quiet person, but at the same time, you really only use your voice when you have something interesting or important to say. That's why you never have trouble getting people to hear your thoughts.

10–16 points
Terrific Talker

Do you ever take a breath? You can have a conversation on just about any topic. While being outgoing is great, don't forget to open your ears, too. Sometimes other people also want to get in a word or two!

Are You TOO DEMANDING?

START

Can you just go with the flow, or do you freak if you don't get your way?

You're at the beach when your friend goes to get you both ice cream. You wanted chocolate; she brought back vanilla. You:

eat it and don't say anything. She went and got it—and ice cream is delicious no matter what.

eat it, but let her know that you really prefer chocolate.

ask her if she's an idiot. You clearly said chocolate.

Your dad buys you a beautiful necklace for your birthday. You'd rather have a bracelet. You:

feel so lucky to have such a thoughtful dad. Maybe you can drop hints about a bracelet for Christmas.

thank him but ask if he'd exchange it for something you really want.

come up with another plan. You don't really care what you do as long as you're all together.

You want to go ice-skating after school. Your friends don't. You:

ask them why they always have to be so difficult!

tell them you'll catch them later.

You're the school social chair and are responsible for decorating the gym for graduation. You asked your committee to buy purple streamers. They got blue instead. You:

Your best friend offers to plan your upcoming birthday party for you. You:

say thanks and then produce a huge list of your likes and dislikes.

feel honored that she'd volunteer to do that for you and can't wait to see what she comes up with.

Your brother won't let you watch what you want on TV. You:

You hate orange juice, yet every morning your mom pours you a glass. Usually you:

hardly notice. Blue and purple are so close in color scheme.

pour it back in the carton. Your mom means well, and just because you hate the sight of it doesn't mean everyone does.

are annoyed, but think you can make it work. You wish they would pay more attention!

are slightly bummed, but hey, at least you're not in school!

groan and leave it there. Maybe someday she'll get the message.

are cool with it. Plans don't always work out. You ask if she has any free days coming up.

LAID-BACK LOVELY

You can roll with any punch and just try to have fun no matter what. Life's too short to sweat the small stuff, so you don't. Your friends and family really appreciate how un-diva-like you are.

You go on a family vacation to the beach, and it rains the whole time. You:

feel sad that you can't go to the beach and hit the shops to make yourself feel better. Surely your parents will understand that if you can't go in the ocean, they'll need to pay for shopping sprees to keep you busy.

whine and complain until your parents agree to go home early.

You made plans with a friend weeks ago, and now she's called to cancel. You:

tell her how disappointed you are and that you were really looking forward to seeing her.

OFTEN EASYGOING

You definitely like things done a certain way, but you try to make the best of a situation. You don't really get worked up over little things, but you will be honest and tell someone if they've disappointed you.

wait until he goes into the kitchen to get a snack and then steal the remote. At least you'll catch a few minutes of your show before he comes back.

start screaming at the top of your lungs until he gives in.

Your sister promised you she would take you to the movies at 5:30 p.m. It's 6 p.m. and she's not home yet. When she arrives and apologizes profusely, you:

let her explain and check the times of the later showings.

insist that her excuse is bogus and that if you were really friends, she'd be able to make it.

refuse to even listen to her excuse. Your time is just as important as hers.

NEVER SATISFIED

You expect a lot from your loved ones, and if they don't deliver, you get very angry. You're not good at spontaneity and want everything to go according to plan. If it doesn't, watch out!

Up-to-speed or Out-of-date?

How in-the-know are you about the world around you?

1 Your social studies teacher announces that she'll be giving weekly current-events quizzes. You:

a. are worried. There is so much going on in the world, how can you keep on top of it all?

b. are psyched. You know what's up in your town and around the world.

c. groan. Now you'll have to start actually paying attention to the news.

2 Your friend is totally in love with the guy who sits behind you in science class. You:

a. make a mental note to find out whether he's single.

b. can't remember what he looks like.

c. rattle off every girl he has ever even passed notes with.

3 A blog is:

a. an online journal where anyone can write about their day-to-day existence.

b. your lifeline. You don't know how you survived before you started one.

c. a scary green monster.

4 The new American Idol is being crowned tonight. You:

a. have already told your friends not to bother you between the hours of 8 and 10 p.m.

b. can't watch, but will definitely tape it for later viewing.

c. have no idea what the show is even about.

5 How do you decide which movie to see?

a. Your movie nights are planned way in advance. You know what movies are opening when, who is starring in them, and all the buzz about them, and you love to be the first in line.

b. Movie trailers on TV usually get you excited for one film over another.

c. You often let your friends pick the movie. You aren't that picky.

6 What year was George W. Bush elected president?

a. Which one is that?

b. 1998

c. 2000

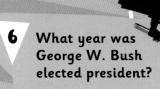

7 At your parents' dinner party, two of the guests start talking about politics. You:

a. listen but don't say anything.

b. join in. You read the newspaper every day.

c. walk away. Politics are a total snooze.

8 Your aunt tells you she's getting a divorce. You:

a. wonder how long she's been married. Were you at the wedding?

b. could have spotted that coming from a mile away. Her husband's a jerk.

c. feel really sorry for her—they've been together a long time.

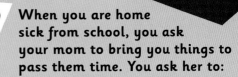

9 When you are home sick from school, you ask your mom to bring you things to pass them time. You ask her to:

a. buy a copy of every celeb rag at the newsstand.

b. rent the entire last season of a TV show that you've heard is good.

c. bring you any old magazines and newspapers lying around the house.

10 Your classmate got in trouble for cheating on a test. You:

a. were the first to hear the news.

b. had no idea he was even in your grade.

c. always thought he was kind of shady.

ANSWERS

1 a=2 b=3 c=1
2 a=2 b=1 c=3
3 a=2 b=3 c=1
4 a=3 b=2 c=1
5 a=3 b=2 c=1
6 a=1 b=2 c=3
7 a=2 b=3 c=1
8 a=1 b=3 c=2
9 a=3 b=2 c=1
10 a=3 b=1 c=2

24–30 points

Up-to-Date Mate

You'd make a great reporter because you always know exactly what's up on your street, in your school, across the country, and around the globe. You read a ton of magazines and newspapers to keep current. Friends rely on you for information.

17–23 points

Paying Attention

You catch the news sometimes and pay attention to what your parents and teachers are talking about, but sometimes, things happen that you don't hear about for a few days. Luckily, you can always hop online if you are wondering about the world.

10–16 points

What's Happening?

Are you living in a bubble? You barely know who the president is! Order a news magazine by mail or sign up online for newspaper alerts so you can get the headlines fast. Pay attention to the world around you. It's an interesting place.

What Is Your PERSONALITY NUMBER?

How other people perceive you can be foretold with a little foray into Numerology.

1 Write your name below

Example: Michelle Ann Hainer

2 Now write down the numbers that correspond to the consonants in your name, using the chart below. Do not use any numbers for the vowels.

1 = J, S	**4** = D, M, V	**7** = G, P, Y
2 = B, K, T	**5** = N, W	**8** = H, Q, Z
3 = C, L	**6** = F, X	**9** = R

Example:

M i c h e l l e
4   38   33

A n n
  5 5

H a i n e r
8   5   9

3 Add up the numbers in each of your names. If the sums have two digits, then keep adding the numbers together until you get a single digit for for each of your names, like this:

Example:

Michelle	Ann	Haine
4+3+8+3+3 = 21	5+5 = 10	8+5+9 = 22
2+1 = 3	1+0 = 1	2+2 = 4

4 Finally, add the totals together. If your total is 11 or 22, do not reduce further, since 11 and 22 are Personality Numbers, too.

Example: 3+1+4 = 8

Your name:	Maia	Rose	Pisani-Konert
Your numbers:	455	91	715 2592
Add them up:	12	10	31
Totals:	3	1	4
Personality Number:		8	

Your Personality Number provides insight into how other people see you. Look below to find out what your Personality Number means for you.

YOU, BY THE NUMBERS

1 You like to take risks and are really creative. You often have your own way of doing things, and people know they can't push you around. Beware of coming off too aggressively or standoffish.

2 You are friendly and gentle, so people feel safe around you. Because you are so good-natured, people may mistake you for a pushover, but you actually have great strength. You are a great listener.

3 You're a ton of fun to be with. You are seen as a party animal, and others recognize your talent for inspiring them. You're also a romantic and fall in love very easily, so you may need to work on creating deeper connections with people.

4 You are really reliable, and people trust you and your judgment. A real family-oriented gal, you're also very frugal and value a dollar, although sometimes people can accuse you of being cheap.

5 You are full of great ideas and are very funny. People are always laughing around you. You're optimistic but can also be a bit impulsive. Try to remember to consider the results of your actions before doing things.

6 You're an extremely compassionate person, and friends often come to you when they need advice. Because you try to see the good in all people, and others know you'll help, you have to try hard not to get tangled up in unwanted drama.

7 You're a bit mysterious, and people never quite know what you're thinking. Most assume you have a serious nature. You are very smart and enjoy studying, but it can be hard for people to get to know you.

8 You are strong both mentally and physically. Others are attracted to your self-assurance but can often be intimidated by you. You have loads of confidence, but you can be ruthless, so try to consider your loved ones' feelings more often.

9 You are graceful and elegant. Perhaps you are a dancer or actress? People are naturally drawn to you. Beware of a tendency to come across as arrogant, because underneath you are very warm and compassionate.

11 You are sensitive and understanding. Maybe you have overcome some level of shyness or maybe you have a secret, but there is something intriguing about you, and others certainly want to figure you out.

22 You are smart and consistent. You want to have an impact on your surroundings and make sure your voice is heard. Others view you as strong and successful. Just make sure you don't get cocky!

77

Are You A GOSSIP?

Do you live to dish the dirt? Or is "mum's the word" more your style?

1 You just heard that the most popular girl in school's dad got arrested for fighting with another father at a football game. You:

  a. feel sorry for her. That must be so hard on her family.

  b. tell your entire circle of friends—and the guys who sit behind you in class.

  c. tell one or two friends what you heard but that you want to make sure it's true.

2 An older student tells you that your science and history teachers are secretly dating. What do you do with this information?

  a. Dish the story at lunchtime. This is too juicy to keep to yourself.

  b. Keep it to yourself. You wouldn't want them to lose their jobs over their romance.

  c. Let your science teacher know that people are talking about her. You really like her and feel like she deserves to know.

3 You just found out that there is a rumor that you kissed a certain boy over the weekend. What do you do?

  a. Nothing. It's not true, and people will stop talking about it more quickly if you don't freak out about it.

  b. Tell your friends to set the record straight to anyone who mentions it

  c. Launch a counterattack. Tell everyone that you heard the same rumor about him with a different girl.

4 Your classmates voted you:

  a. "Most Loyal."

  b. "Most Likely to Succeed."

  c. "Most Talkative."

5 Rumor has it that the star ballerina in your dance class has an eating disorder. You:

  a. offer her a cookie. When she declines, tell your friends that's proof she has a problem.

  b. let her know that if she ever needs to talk, you're there to listen.

  c. ignore the comments. People are just jealous of her because she's so good.

6 You accidentally saw your teacher's grade book —and all of the people who are failing. You:

a. tell your best friend that neither of you has anything to worry about. Phew!

b. gleefully let the news fly. One of the flunkies is a guy who made fun of you all year!

c. try to forget, although you're thankful you aren't one of them.

7 Everyone in school thinks the new girl is secretly a witch. You know that she's just shy and lonely. The next time someone talks about her in front of you, you:

a. say nothing. It's such a silly story that it isn't hurting anyone.

b. tell them they're being ridiculous. Just because someone is quiet doesn't mean that they are up to something. They'd realize that if they just talked to her.

c. remark how you thought you saw her holding a voodoo doll and chanting a spell in the locker room.

8 You're on the phone with Amy but hang up when you see Sarah calling on the other line. How much of your conversation with Amy do you tell Sarah?

a. All of it, word for word

b. Some of it. Amy's finally got a date with Josh. She won't care if you tell Sarah.

c. None of it. You don't break confidences.

9 People know they can always count on you:

a. to keep a secret.

b. for information. You know everything and everyone in town.

c. to invite them to a cool party.

ANSWERS

1 a=1 b=3 c=2
2 a=3 b=1 c=2
3 a=1 b=2 c=3
4 a=1 b=2 c=3
5 a=3 b=2 c=1
6 a=2 b=3 c=1
7 a=1 b=2 c=3
8 a=3 b=2 c=1
9 a=1 b=3 c=2

22–27 points
DISHING DIVA

If you come into a juicy piece of gossip, you better believe you're going to share it! Everyone loves hearing your latest scoop, but eventually they may have trouble trusting you when they realize that you probably talk about them, too.

16–21 points
TRUTH TALKER

You don't spread many rumors— at least not until you can confirm that they're true. You do love to listen to gossip, though. It's exciting and, for the most part, it's harmless. Who knew other people's lives were so exciting?

9–15 points
ZIPPED LIPS

You hate the rumor mill at school and do everything you can to avoid being a part of it. Gossip hurts people, and you're just not into that. Besides, you would be heartbroken if you found out that someone was spreading tales about you.

What Is Your Secret Strength?

Everyone's got some special quality that makes him or her powerful and unique. Find out yours.

3 **When you grow up, you think you might like to:**

a. be a teacher.

b. be a community activist.

c. be a judge or lawyer.

d. work with the disabled.

1 **The family dog dies, and your sister is devastated. You:**

a. tell her it's for the best. He was old and sick. He'd had a long, full life.

b. write a poem to recite at Fido's funeral.

c. consider getting a fish. You can't go through this again.

d. cry with her as you reminisce about the good times both of you had with Fido.

4 **You pride yourself on:**

a. being good in a crisis.

b. your honesty.

c. seeing more than one side to every issue.

d. being able to make people feel better.

2 **Your mom gets a new job, and you have to move to another state. You:**

a. look at the move as an opportunity to start fresh and meet new people.

b. set up cameras on your and your best friend's computers so you can make video phone calls once a week.

c. realize that your parents are really going to need your help in the coming months.

d. never let your parents see how miserable you are. On top of all the stress, you don't want them to feel bad for you.

5 **Your favorite extracurricular activity is:**

a. filming school news segments.

b. soccer.

c. drama club.

d. volunteering at an animal shelter.

6 **Your greatest fear is:**

a. being attacked by an animal.

b. losing all of your friends.

c. going blind or deaf.

d. getting your heart broken.

7 **If you could have a super power, what would you choose?**

a. Flying

b. Invisibility

c. X-ray vision

d. Extendable arms and legs

8 **If you could change one thing about yourself, you'd:**

a. be more outgoing.

b. be more impulsive.

c. be less sensitive.

d. take more time for yourself.

Answers

Mostly A's
Calm As Can Be

Nothing rattles you, and you know what to do in any situation. Your cool-headedness is much appreciated by everyone around you. If there was ever a huge crisis in your town, friends would want you with them for comfort.

Mostly B's
True Blue Loyal Lady

A tried-and-true friend, you'll always be there for your crew. Even if someone betrays you, you'll forgive them, because you understand the value of friendship. Your family can always count on you.

Mostly C's
Perfectly Perceptive

You really pay attention to how people's actions affect others and are a great judge of character. You easily uncover people's true intentions and can spot a fake friend a mile away. You have a great memory and an eye for detail.

Mostly D's
Completely Compassionate

You're an emotional being, and you know instinctively when a friend needs you. There is no better shoulder than yours to cry on. You're kind-hearted and patient and treat your fellow human beings with grace and respect.

What Does Your DRAWING Mean?

Draw a picture of a tree in the space to the right. To decipher your drawing and reveal its hidden meaning, check out the upside down questions below.

Is your tree centered in the box? If so, you are a very confident person.

Does your tree have apples on it? If so, you are a person who loves to be nurtured and looked after.

Does the tree have roots? If you drew roots to your tree, you are a grounded person who feels well loved. A rootless tree or one whose base does not look wide enough to hold up the tree may mean that you feel lost or insecure.

How big are the branches? If they are large, heavy braches, it may be hard for you to say no to people. You may take on too many activities or too much responsibility and neglect yourself in the process. Small branches may mean that you're a bit selfish and aren't really interested in helping others. Twisted branches could mean you are struggling with an inner conflict.

Does your tree have leaves? Drawing lots of leaves on your tree means you are a good communicator. If the leaves have fallen off your tree, it could mean that you are feeling empty or sad about something.

How wide is the tree trunk? If it's skinny, it might mean that you're feeling unsatisfied with your life right now and are looking for something to make you happy. If the trunk is wide and sturdy, you have a lot of inner strength.

Where Will You and Your Honey Honeymoon?

So you've had the fancy wedding. But now where will you spend the first weeks of married life?

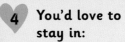

1 You and your husband met:

a. at the gym.

b. at a trendy restaurant.

c. at a cooking class.

2 As a couple, you two will probably spend a lot of time:

a. outdoors, hiking, and biking.

b. checking out new buzz-worthy restaurants.

c. throwing parties and hosting dinners with friends.

3 You both love to eat:

a. burritos.

b. sushi.

c. pasta.

4 You'd love to stay in:

a. a cozy cabin.

b. a five-star hotel.

c. a medieval castle.

5 You want your honeymoon to be filled with:

a. exhilarating activities.

b. relaxation and pampering.

c. museums, artwork, and historical sightseeing.

6 Both you and your hubby will:

a. have adventurous spirits.

b. always get invited to the best parties and events.

c. love to learn about different cultures.

ANSWERS

Mostly A's
Worldwide Trek

Hiking in Nepal, mountain climbing in Morocco, or scuba diving in Cozumel are perfect getaways for you and your thrill-seeking partner. Both of you hate to sit still and love being active. Simply going to the beach would be a bore for you.

Mostly B's
Deluxe Ocean Oasis

Monaco, Martinique, St. Tropez—whatever destination is the latest playground for the rich and famous is where you'll be headed. Lovers of luxury, you two will spend your days by the pool and your nights at trendy clubs.

Mostly C's
European Getaway

You and your new husband want to soak up new art, architecture, cuisine, and customs on your honeymoon. In Italy, France, or Spain, you'll spend your days marveling at beautiful works of art and canoodling at charming outdoor cafes.

Do You THINK Too Much?

Do you pick apart every little thing to see if it has a hidden meaning?

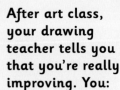

1 Your crush mentioned that he might be hanging out at the movies tonight. You:

a. wonder if that means he wants you to join him.

b. assume he told you only so you'll know he already has other plans.

c. plan on going to the movies, too.

2 Your mom asks you if you want peanut butter ice cream or mint chocolate chip. You:

a. pick a flavor immediately. It'll be mint chocolate chip.

b. want a little of both.

c. have a tough time deciding. You really want the mint chocolate chip... although it has been a while since you've had peanut butter... but you really love mint ice cream.

3 Your friend Stephanie tells you she's taking your other friend Anna with her on her family vacation. You:

a. wonder if she's telling you this to make you jealous.

b. feel a little bit hurt that you're not invited, but you did go on vacation with Stephanie's family last year.

c. tell them to have a great time.

4 You're taking a quiz in math class, and the teacher gives you 30 minutes to complete it. How long do you take?

a. No more than 10 minutes

b. 15 to 20 minutes

c. The whole 30 and then ask your teacher for an extra 5 to check it over for the 14th time

5 After art class, your drawing teacher tells you that you're really improving. You:

a. float home on her compliment. You've been working hard.

b. are sure she meant you were really bad before.

c. ask her in what areas she thinks you've gotten better.

7 Your principal tells your parents that you'll make a great politician someday. You:

a. take that as sign that he thinks you're a great leader.

b. think he probably meant that in a good way… didn't he?

c. aren't sure how to take that. Is he saying you're dishonest? Or that you are persuasive? Maybe he's saying that you talk too much?

8 You don't get invited to a classmate's party. You:

a. think maybe your Evite® got lost in cyberspace or something.

b. aren't surprised. You're not really friends.

c. start thinking back to whether you may have said something to offend her.

9 Your grandmother tells you that you look like you've lost weight. You:

a. think she is trying to tell you that you looked really fat the last time you saw her.

b. say thanks—you have been going to the gym.

c. make a mental note of the outfit that you are wearing so that you can wear it whenever you want to look good.

6 You have to write an essay about your reactions to a book you read in English class. How many drafts does it take to get it right?

a. At least three—you want to make sure you've covered every angle.

b. Drafts? You just type up whatever comes to mind.

c. Two. You type it and then check to make sure it makes sense and that you didn't forget any punctuation.

ANSWERS

1 a=3 b=2 c=1
2 a=1 b=2 c=3
3 a=3 b=2 c=1
4 a=1 b=2 c=3
5 a=1 b=3 c=2
6 a=3 b=1 c=2
7 a=1 b=2 c=3
8 a=2 b=1 c=3
9 a=3 b=1 c=2

21–27 Points
TOTAL OVERTHINKER

Oh my! How do you have time to do anything fun when you spend so much time agonizing over decisions and second-guessing other people's motives? Relax and try to take people at face value. You will save a lot of time and stress. Plus, it's often more fun to just go with the flow.

15–20 points
SOMETIME SECOND-GUESSER

You try not to be overly sensitive, but sometimes you can't help but wonder if people really mean what they say. This is especially true of guys you like and girls whom you don't know very well. You also know that you can drive yourself nuts if you read too much into everyone's words.

9–14 points
NOT A SECOND THOUGHT

You don't believe in overanalyzing things. When someone speaks to you, you process what he or she says and move on. You're good at making decisions, and you know what you want—and what you don't. You don't want to waste your time agonizing over the comments of others.

EARTH, WIND, FIRE, or WATER?

Which element describes you best? See what this quiz reveals.

1 A friend bets you $50 that she can beat you at a game of cards. You:

a. don't accept. Fifty bucks is a lot of money.

b. gladly agree. You'll show her who's boss!

c. agree to $20, but to make it interesting, suggest playing three games. Two out of three wins.

d. tell her you would rather play cards for fun than for money.

2 If you inherited a large sum of money, you'd:

a. buy a house.

b. take a ton of vacations and buy new clothes whenever you want.

c. invest it in the stock market.

d. donate half to good causes like breast cancer research, battered women's shelters, and famine relief.

3 Two of your best friends get into a huge fight. It's your job to:

a. stay out of it. You love them both and don't want to take sides.

b. tell them they're both being stubborn, and they should just get over themselves.

c. invite them both to lunch and don't let them leave until they've made up.

d. listen to each side of the argument and try to calm them down enough to talk it out.

4 It's opening night of the school play. You're the lead. Before you take the stage, you:

a. take a last moment to look over your lines.

b. give the cast a group hug.

c. take a deep breath to help your concentration.

d. throw up.

5 You don't like people who:

a. constantly do silly things for attention.

b. don't speak their minds.

c. only care about themselves.

d. are mean or rude to other people.

6 What is your astrological sign?

a. Taurus, Virgo, Capricorn

b. Aries, Leo, Sagittarius

c. Gemini, Libra, Aquarius

d. Cancer, Scorpio, Pisces

7 Your mom lets you buy one thing at the mall. What do you choose?

a. A pair of black pants that fit perfectly

b. A sparkly tank top

c. A silver necklace

d. A new diary to record your thoughts in

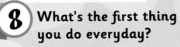

8 What's the first thing you do everyday?

a. Eat a healthy breakfast

b. Brush your unruly hair

c. Splash water on your face and think about the day to come

d. Lie in bed, trying to remember any dreams you had in the night

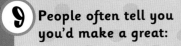

9 People often tell you you'd make a great:

a. lawyer.

b. television reporter.

c. social worker.

d. psychologist.

ANSWERS

Mostly A's
EARTH

You're a very practical, grounded person. You don't like to take risks, yet you love to acquire new possessions. Some may think that you are materialistic, but you see money or objects as proof that your hard work pays off.

Mostly B's
FIRE

You're outgoing, enthusiastic, and can definitely cause a stir wherever you go. People love being around you, although you can be a bit bossy sometimes and have a fiery temper. You have lots of friends and are very creative.

Mostly C's
WIND

You're calm, super-smart, and a really good speaker. An idealist, you want to make the world a better place and are always able to see both sides of a situation. But you can be cold and distant when someone upsets you.

Mostly D's
WATER

You're a sensitive person. Even if you don't always let people know it, you feel things deeply, which means that you can be easily hurt by insensitive people. You are extremely caring and compassionate in friendship.

What Kind of MaKeover Do You Need?

You've just won a reality show, and the prize is a makeover of your choice. Where do you need a little help?

1 You spend a lot of time thinking about:

a. homework.

b. the flat-screen TV you want.

c. what you're going to wear.

d. your friends.

2 If you could change one thing about yourself, you'd:

a. be less stressed out.

b. sleep more.

c. highlight your hair.

d. talk about people less.

3 You argue with your parents frequently about:

a. your future.

b. why they won't let you paint your room green.

c. your appearance. They hate your ripped jeans.

d. how much time you spend on the phone.

4 You've got a week's vacation from school. What are you planning on doing?

a. Relaxing in front of the TV. You don't want to do anything that requires thinking.

b. Making a photo collage for your bedroom

c. Reorganizing your closet

d. Logging in some alone time. You need a break.

5 You earn $100 helping your neighbor rake her yard all weekend. What do you spend it on?

a. A luxurious spa day

b. A super-comfy chair for your room

c. Sassy new shoes

d. Dinner out with your best friend

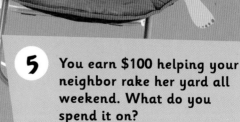

6 **You never feel like you have enough time to:**

a. study before tests.

b. just hang out and do nothing.

c. get ready for school in the morning.

d. call, IM, or email everyone who contacts you.

7 **Your dad gets a new job and your family has to move across the country. When you look on the bright side, what do you think about the move?**

a. "At least you'll never have to be in mean Mrs. Matthews' class again! She's a nightmare!"

b. "Maybe my new room will be bigger than my old one."

c. "This is a chance to reinvent myself. Punk rock girl perhaps?"

d. "It'll be nice to meet a bunch of new people."

8 **You come home from school in a really bad mood. What's got you so upset?**

a. You did not make the varsity soccer team.

b. You're just really bored at home with no one to hang out with.

c. Another girl showed up wearing the exact same outfit you had on.

d. You found out one of your "friends" has been flirting with your crush.

9 **At lunch, you often sit with:**

a. whoever has room at their table.

b. your best friend.

c. a different person each day.

d. your core group of five girlfriends.

ANSWERS

Mostly A's
SCHOOL RETOOL
It sounds like school—and all the tests, homework, and popularity contests that go with it—have really got you down. A school makeover to get you excited about education is what you need!

Mostly B's
ROOM REDO
OK, so maybe purple bunny rabbit wallpaper was cute when you were four, but it's soooo babyish now. You need a room that reflects who you are today. It is time to reboot your bedroom.

Mostly C's
FASHION FIX UP
You've got cute style, but it's just like everyone else's. You're sick of all of your clothes and would die to get rid of everything and get a whole new wardrobe. Now's your chance!

Mostly D's
SOCIAL RESTART
You love your friends, you really do. But sometimes, you get fed up with them. It happens, especially if you spend every moment together. You need to join new clubs and meet new people.

Who's Your DREAM Date?

What kind of hunk is your perfect match?

1 You're usually drawn to guys who:

a. are really hot.

b. love to help others.

c. have a great sense of humor.

d. are a little bit moody and mysterious.

2 You like it when a guy wears:

a. designer clothes.

b. ripped jeans and T-shirts.

c. Hawaiian shirts.

d. anything black.

3 You're at the beach together. While you catch some rays, what's he doing?

a. Laying out with you. He's a sun worshipper, too.

b. Teaching your little brother to swim

c. Attempting to ride a Jet Ski®

d. Sitting under an umbrella reading

4 A guy would have your heart forever if he:

a. wrote you a song.

b. could teach you to look at the world in a different way.

c. made you smile and laugh so much your cheeks ached.

d. told you a secret about himself.

5 A perfect evening would include:

a. hitting the hottest clubs.

b. volunteering at a music benefit for West Africa.

c. watching a ton of comedies on DVD and ordering Chinese food.

d. going to a poetry reading.

6 You have a huge crush on a guy you met:

a. at the mall.

b. at a peace march.

c. at the ice cream parlor where you work.

d. at a concert.

7 You walk by your crush when he's hanging out with his friends. When you nod hello, he:

a. smiles and winks at you.

b. introduces you to his buds.

c. pretends to trip on something to make you laugh.

d. stares intently at you until you blush.

8 How many girlfriends has he had?

a. A couple of long-term ones

b. Too many to count

c. None

d. You have no idea

ANSWERS

Mostly A's
ROMANTIC ROMEO

You like a guy who is well dressed, knows where the good parties are, and is incredibly hot. You love to be showered with flowers, perfume, chocolates, and cuddly stuffed animals.

Mostly B's
HUNK WITH A HEART OF GOLD

Looks are definitely a plus, but you also want your guy to be socially conscious and into helping others. There's a lot of work to be done in the world, and you want to tackle it together.

Mostly C's
COMICAL CUTIE

You want a guy who is fun and is always the life of the party. Being able to be goofy and laugh is really important to you. You don't care about looks so much if your guy always keeps you entertained.

Mostly D's
QUIRKY CASANOVA

You like unique, artsy guys who always keep you guessing. Mysterious guys have a lot going on in their brains, and you always want to find out more about them. Plus, they can introduce you to completely new cultural experiences.

Predict Your Friend's FUTURE

Make copies of this quiz to give to your friends—or read the sentences out loud. Then fill out the questions below for both you and her. When you're done, swap quizzes and see how psychic you really are.

All About My Friend:

_____ (her name)

1. Someday, she will kiss _____ (name)

2. She will get an A in _____ (class)

3. At graduation, she will be voted most likely to _____

4. She will study or work abroad in _____ (city or country)

5. Her first job will be _____ (job title)

6. She will always play _____ (sport)

7. She will meet her future husband at _____

8. She will know her husband for _____ (amount of time) before they get married.

All About Me:

_____ (your name)

1. Someday, I will kiss _____ (name)

2. I will get an A in _____ (class)

3. At graduation, I will be voted most likely to _____

4. I will study or work abroad in _____ (city or country)

5. My first job will be _____ (job title)

6. I will always play _____ (sport)

7. I will meet my future husband at _____

8. I will know my husband for _____ (amount of time)
   before we get married .

9. I will honeymoon in _____ (location) .

10. I will have _____ (number) kids.

11. One day, I will meet _____ (famous person) .

12. I will travel to _____ (location) .

13. _____ will be my prized possession .

14. My greatest accomplishment will be _____ .

15. When I retire, I will _____

9. She will honeymoon in _____ (location) .

10. She will have _____ (number) kids .

11. One day, she will meet _____ (famous person) .

12. She will travel to _____ (location) .

13. _____ will be her prized possession .

14. Her greatest accomplishment will be _____

15. When she retires,
    she will _____

YOUR SCORE: Now give yourself one point for each match.

11–15 points
FUTURE FORTUNE-TELLER
You know your friend really well, so it's no wonder that you see the future the same way she does. Look back at this in twenty years and see how much of it comes true!

6–10 points
SORTA PSYCHIC
You're on the same wavelength when it comes to some future events, although you don't agree on every twist and turn. But hey, the future is up for grabs, and anything can happen!

0–5 points
CAN'T BE CLAIRVOYANT
You tried to see into the future, but you didn't do so well. Don't sweat it though! Not everyone has the psychic touch. Keep in contact as you grow older to see which one of you guessed better!

What Is Your Legacy?

When high school becomes a thing of the past, how will you be remembered?

1 It's a Saturday afternoon. What are you doing?

a. Practicing your solo for next week's school talent show

b. Studying for a killer biology test

c. Volunteering at the local senior citizen's center

2 You fantasize about being:

a. rich and famous.

b. the president of the United States.

c. the person who puts an end to hunger in Africa.

3 You want people to respect you for your:

a. talent.

b. intelligence.

c. big heart.

4 Your friends come to you when they:

a. can't decide what to wear.

b. need help with their homework.

c. want someone to listen to their troubles.

5 Big crowds:

a. excite you beyond belief.

b. can make you a little nervous.

c. aren't your thing at all.

6 You have two sisters. You're considered the:

a. loud one.

b. smart one.

c. responsible one.

94

7 You overhear your best friend describing you to another friend that you've never met. What does she say?

a. "She is beautiful and full of life. I know she is going to be famous someday."

b. "She is the smartest person I know—and one of the nicest."

c. "She is a total sweetheart who would do anything for her friends. She is always helping people out."

8 Every summer, you:

a. go to theater camp.

b. read tons of books.

c. work at a summer camp.

9 You're most proud of the fact that you:

a. got picked to sing the National Anthem at a local ball game.

b. were the class valedictorian.

c. helped a group of struggling youngsters with their reading.

ANSWERS

Mostly A's
Star Style
You'd be voted Most Likely to Have Her Own Talk Show. When people think of you, they automatically remember your charm, grace, and incredible talent. Singing, dancing, acting—you can do it all. You'll be entertaining the crowds for a long time to come.

Mostly B's
Super Smarts
You'd be voted Most Likely to Win a Nobel Prize. You're going to accomplish big things in the world. Whether your field is medicine, economics, or literature, you'll always strive to push yourself to new heights—and you'll be recognized for your awesome brainpower.

Mostly C's
Helping Hand
You'd be voted Most Likely to Change the World. You're completely selfless and really want to help people. You've already done so much to bring joy to people's lives and that's only the beginning. Your good works will be worthy of sainthood someday!

Photo Credits

DK Publishing would like to thank the following for their kind permission to reproduce their photographs:

COVER: Lori Martin/BigStockPhoto.com (iPod), Angela Coppola © DK Publishing (pink hat), www.Shutterstock.com (soccer ball), Elpiniki/iStockphoto.com (easel); **2-3:** www.Shutterstock.com (horse, shoes, weights, megaphone, pink chair), Anastasiya Maksymenko/iStockphoto.com (laptop), Angela Coppola © DK Publishing (bracelets), Christine Balderas/iStockphoto.com (ice cream cones); **4-5:** www.Shutterstock.com (skirt), Steven Tulissi/iStockphoto.com (keys), Andres Rodriguez/iStockphoto.com (car), Angela Coppola © DK Publishing (necklace); **6-7:** Susi Bikle/iStockphoto.com (rain boot), www.Shutterstock.com (crutches), Stephen Oliver © Dorling Kindersley (ballet shoes); **8-9:** Eileen Meyer/BigStockPhoto.com (shoes), Alanis Laredo/BigStockPhoto.com (bouquet), Morozova Simferpol/BigStockPhoto.com (wedding dress); **10-11:** Stephen Oliver © Dorling Kindersley (sand and shells), www.Shutterstock.com (red ribbon, party hat, noisemaker); **12-13:** Louis Aguinaldo/iStockphoto.com (bikini); **14-15:** Mat Barrand/iStockphoto.com (knitting), Ricardo Isotton/iStockphoto.com (pool), www.Shutterstock.com (purse); **16-17:** Bonita Hein/iStockphoto.com (index cards), Chris Wynia/iStockphoto.com (ski goggles); **18-19:** Angela Coppola © DK Publishing (soccer bag, purple purse, alligator purse), Mark Aplet/iStockphoto.com (red backpack), Nicholas Monu/iStockphoto.com (red purse); **20-21:** Louis Aguinaldo/iStockphoto.com (jeans skirt), Carolina K. Smith/Dreamstime (bra), Lanica Klein/iStockphoto.com (blue lockers); **22-23:** www.Shutterstock.com (chairs); **24-25:** Rafa Irusta/iStockphoto.com (shopping bags); **26-27:** TexasMary/iStockphoto.com (SUV), Lis Gagne/iStockphoto.com (convertible), Andres Rodriguez/iStockphoto.com (green car), Steven Tulissi/iStockphoto.com (keys), www.Shutterstock.com (roses, Eiffel Tower); **28-29:** www.Shutterstock.com (recycling bins); **30-31:** www.Shutterstock.com (spooky mansion); **32-33:** Angela Coppola © DK Publishing (headband), www.Shutterstock.com (skirt); **34-35:** www.Shutterstock.com; **36-37:** Verna Bice/BigStockPhoto.com (palette), www.Shutterstock.com (iPod, statue); **38-39:** www.Shutterstock.com (red, blue, and turquoise bags; black and white bag; star; director's chair); **40-41:** Ben Goode/Dreamstime (TV), www.Shutterstock.com (film reels); **44-45:** Edyta Pawłowska/iStockphoto.com (coin purse), www.Shutterstock.com (window, megaphone); **46-47:** Angela Coppola © DK Publishing (hair accessories), www.Shutterstock.com (hair clippers, comb, and scissors), Route 66 Photography/BigStockPhoto.com (clown); **48-49:** www.Shutterstock.com (remote control), Kelly Cline/iStockphoto.com (sandwich); **50-51:** www.Shutterstock.com (soccer ball and gloves, ring box); **52-53:** www.Shutterstock.com (snowboarder, tree); **54-55:** www.Shutterstock.com (phone, trophy), Scott Rothstein/Dreamstime (locket); **56-57:** Angela Coppola © DK Publishing (all hats), Aldra/iStockphoto.com (spa woman), www.Shutterstock.com (Mount Everest), Bruce Lonngren/iStockphoto.com (crystal ball); **58-59:** www.Shutterstock.com (chocolate ice cream), Kian Khoun Tan/BigStockPhoto.com (iPod); **60-61:** www.Shutterstock.com (leopard-print heels, skirt, black shirt, blue shirt, jeans, pile of clothes, boots, white and pink sneakers, green shoes), Angela Coppola © DK Publishing (belt, bracelets, flip-flops, sunglasses, necklace, earrings), Laura Barrett/BigStockPhoto.com (red shoes); **62-63:** Lucato/iStockphoto.com (pool); **64-65:** Max Blain/iStockphoto.com (cupcakes); **66-67:** Vladimir Mucibabic/iStockphoto.com (lemonade); **68-69:** www.Shutterstock.com (horse, hot-air balloon), Tom Lewis/iStockphoto.com (canoe); **70-71:** Tina Rencelj/iStockphoto.com (phone), www.Shutterstock.com (pizza, loudspeaker); **72-73:** Christine Balderas/iStockphoto.com (ice cream cones), Angela Coppola © DK Publishing (necklace), www.Shutterstock.com (remote control); **74-75:** Anastasiya Maksymenko/iStockphoto.com (laptop); **76-77:** Cecelia Lim/iStockphoto.com (party hat), Stephen Oliver © Dorling Kindersley (ballet shoes), www.Shutterstock.com (weights); **78-79:** www.Shutterstock.com (girl, kiss mark); **80-81:** Stephen Oliver © Dorling Kindersley (soccer ball); **82-83:** www.Shutterstock.com (exercise bike); **84-85:** www.Shutterstock.com (scale); **86-87:** www.Shutterstock.com (boxing gloves); **88-89:** www.Shutterstock.com (chair), Thomasz Pietryszek/iStockphoto.com (truck); **90-91:** www.Shutterstock.com (Chinese food container); **92-93:** www.Shutterstock.com (graduation cap); **94-95:** www.Shutterstock.com (diploma, books, marks, limo), Alex Gumerov/iStockphoto.com (paparazzi); **BACK COVER:** Stephen Oliver © Dorling Kindersley (candy), Angela Coppola © DK Publishing (white gloves), www.Shutterstock.com (ballet shoes, butterfly, chair).

All other images © Dorling Kindersley.
For further information, see www.dkimages.com.